The Cognitive Demo:

Designing Software Presentations That Match How the Brain Learns

By Jeff Mildon

Printed in the United States of America
ISBN: 978-1-968360-10-8
Imprint: MiltyMedia

First Printing, 202

Contents

Introduction

Why Demos Fail — And What Brain Science Can Do About It

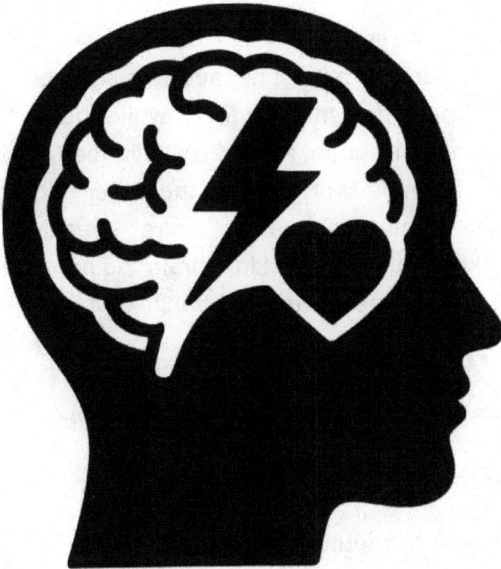

You're mid-demo. The software is running smoothly. Your delivery is polished. And yet... the energy is off. Your audience isn't nodding. Questions are scarce. You wrap up, and the prospect says, "Thanks, we'll be in touch."
Two weeks later, the deal is dead.

Sound familiar?

If you've worked in software sales, this scene is more than common; it's a weekly ritual. Great products fall flat. Polished presentations land with a thud. And sales teams are left wondering: What went wrong?

The truth is this: Most demos fail not because the software is weak, but because the demo is designed for logic, while the audience is operating in emotion, distraction, and mental overload. Traditional demos present to the mind that we wish the buyer had—a calm, focused, receptive brain. In reality, we're speaking to an overstimulated, skeptical, multitasking brain doing its best to survive the workday. This book is here to change that.

The Problem Isn't the Software. It's the Human Brain.

Most salespeople are taught to prepare demos by asking:

- What features should I show?

- What pain points should I address?

- What success stories should I insert?

These are good questions, but they ignore a more important one: What is the brain on the receiving end capable of absorbing, remembering, and acting on, right now?

The brain is not a sponge. It has limits. And most demos exceed them within five minutes.

We overload working memory.

We ignore cognitive biases.

We trigger emotional resistance without knowing it.

The result? Even great demos slide off the brain like water off Teflon.

A Demo Is a Learning Experience—Not a Product Tour

Here's the radical truth at the core of this book:

A sales demo is not a pitch. It's a learning experience.

When you demo software, your audience must learn new systems, understand abstract workflows, map them to their world, and believe in your value in one sitting. That's not just persuasion. That's cognitive transformation.

To make that happen, you need more than product knowledge. You need to understand:

- How attention works.

- How the brain handles overload.

- How emotion impacts retention.

- How prior knowledge shapes perception.

This book will give you that knowledge—and the practical tools to apply it in every call.

The Rise of the "Cognitive Seller"

A new kind of seller is emerging, one who understands that every deal begins in the mind of the buyer. This seller doesn't just memorize product features. They study how people think, learn, and decide. They design presentations that work with the brain's natural patterns, not against them. We call this person a Cognitive Seller. And their secret weapon is the Cognitive Demo.

This book is your blueprint for becoming that kind of seller. Each chapter builds on research from:

- Cognitive psychology

- Instructional design

- Behavioral economics

- Neuroscience   of   learning

And this book translates the above terms into tactical moves you can use on your very next demo.

What You'll Learn in This Book

Here's what you'll walk away with:

- Why your audience forgets most demos, and how to make yours stick

- How to structure your presentation to fit the brain's memory curve

- How to reduce cognitive load and increase perceived simplicity

- How to use storytelling, visuals, and timing to lock in attention

- How to overcome emotional resistance and "mental objections"

- How to run better demos for executives, mixed stakeholders, and remote environments

- And how to scale this method across your team

This is not a theory book. Every concept comes with real-world examples, case studies, and step-by-step strategies. Whatever your role in the sales process, this book will change the way you think about presenting software forever.

The Future of Demos Is Brain-Aligned

In the noisy, crowded world of software sales, attention is a limited currency. Demos that don't honor the way people actually learn and decide are not just ineffective, they're invisible. The future belongs to those who understand how the brain works—and design for it.

Welcome to the Cognitive Demo.

Let's begin.

Chapter 1: Prospect's Brain - Not a Blank Slate

Understanding the invisible psychology shaping your software demo.

Section 1: The Illusion of the Rational Buyer

Sales professionals often prepare demos assuming the audience is a rational evaluator, someone comparing features, weighing costs, and making a logical decision. But in reality, buyers are more like chaotic weather systems than calculating computers.

Neuroscience reveals that over 90% of decision-making happens subconsciously, governed by emotional triggers, memory shortcuts, and instinctive preferences. Nobel laureate Daniel Kahneman separates our minds into two systems:

- System 1 is fast, emotional, and intuitive.

- System 2 is slower, more rational, and effortful.

Here's the catch: System 1 is always in charge first. So, when your demo begins, your audience is not analyzing; it's reacting.

Real-World Example:

During a live demo for a financial software suite, a sales engineer opened with a feature-rich dashboard. Half the room immediately became disengaged. Why? It triggered overwhelm. The visual complexity activated System 1's alarm bells. By the time System 2 tried to engage, the audience had already checked out.

The lesson? Your demo needs to court emotion before it can appeal to logic.

Section 2: Mental Models Matter More Than You Think

Mental models are deeply ingrained expectations about how things should work. In software sales, aligning with a prospect's mental model makes the demo feel "right." Violating it, even with a better solution, causes confusion and resistance.

Case Scenario:

Imagine you're demoing a project management tool. The client is used to linear Gantt charts. Your software uses a Kanban board. It's more modern, flexible, and user-friendly. But halfway through your demo, the VP frowns and says, "This feels chaotic." Why? You've disrupted her mental model.

The solution is to bridge the model:

- Start by showing how your system replicates the key benefits of Gantt.

- Then transition to why Kanban provides faster visibility and collaboration.

By validating the existing structure first, you earn permission to evolve it.

Section 3: Prior Knowledge is the Anchor of Attention

Your prospect doesn't begin learning at zero. They come armed with analogies, references, past software experiences, and organizational quirks. Good demos activate this knowledge. Great demos connect to it.

According to cognitive theorists, new information "sticks" best when:

1. It connects to something known.

2. It's delivered in a way that allows application.

3. It's emotionally relevant.

Your job in a demo is to activate familiarity first. For example:

- Say, "This works like Excel, but..."

- Or, "If you've used Salesforce, think of this as the admin version."

These mental hooks build a cognitive scaffold for what's coming next.

Section 4: Prospect Stress is the Hidden Demo Saboteur

Cognitive scientists describe stress as a performance suppressor. Under stress, the brain diverts resources away from the prefrontal cortex, the center for reasoning, and toward survival instincts. In demo terms, this means:

- Prospects forget details.

- They misinterpret UI labels.

- They resist change reflexively.

Hidden Stress Triggers During Demos:

- Feeling like they "should get this" but don't.

- Worrying about how they'll explain the product to their boss.

- Fearing that adopting your solution will expose inefficiencies in their team.

Begin your demo by lowering anxiety:

- Clarify what's coming: "I'll show you 3 quick workflows, then we'll go deeper."

- Normalize confusion: "Don't worry if something's new. This is meant to spark ideas, not be an exam."

- Show a quick win early.

Section 5: Cognitive Biases That Shape Every Demo

Every demo passes through a filter of invisible biases. Here are a few that affect interpretation:

- Anchoring Bias: The first thing shown sets the tone. Start with a clunky admin panel, and the whole tool feels clunky.

- Confirmation Bias: Prospects look for proof that aligns with their pre-existing beliefs about tools, industries, or vendors.

- Loss Aversion: Prospects will resist change if they perceive a loss in control, familiarity, or autonomy—even if the gain is large.

Tactical Tip:

If a prospect previously used a competing tool, never trash it. Instead, reframe:

"What you're used to is great at X. We've taken that foundation and optimized it for Y."

Section 6: The Reticular Activating System and Demo Relevance

The Reticular Activating System (RAS) is the brain's filter for relevance. It decides what to ignore and what to spotlight—often based on goals, survival, or emotional triggers.

Your job in a demo is to trigger the RAS early and often:

- Use role-specific language: "As a billing coordinator, here's what you'll love..."

- Tie features to emotions: "This part eliminates end-of-month panic."

- Ask framing questions: "If you could wave a magic wand over this workflow, what would vanish?"

The more relevant the message, the more likely the brain is to remember—and act on—it.

Section 7: A Multi-Brain Room—When One Demo Has Many Minds

Rarely do you demo to just one stakeholder. Each role brings its own cognitive filter:

- Executives care about strategic value and risk.

- Users care about task flow and friction.

- IT cares about integration, security, and scale.

One demo = multiple brains = multiple learning paths.

The Fix:

Instead of trying to impress everyone at once, signal to each group:

- "For leadership, you'll see real-time impact dashboards…"

- "For frontline users, here's the workflow that saves 90 minutes per day…"

- "And IT, note the API layer that simplifies provisioning."

This cognitive cueing ensures everyone stays engaged.

Section 8: Stories as Cognitive Shortcuts

Stories are neural superhighways. The brain is wired to absorb, store, and recall stories far better than raw data or interface walkthroughs.

Replace statements like:

"This module helps manage tickets."

With:

"Let me tell you about a client who had 300 backlogged tickets. This view helped them triage by priority within an hour—and by day's end, their first-response time was cut in half."

This moves the brain from evaluating software to experiencing the solution—a huge shift in retention and persuasion.

Section 9: When the Demo Confirms Fears Instead of Eases Them

Some prospects aren't afraid that your software won't work. They're afraid that it will! And, in doing so, will force uncomfortable change.

For instance:

1. Automation may threaten job security.

2. Centralized systems may reduce autonomy.

3. Transparency may expose inefficiencies.

If your demo reinforces those fears, you'll see subtle resistance:

- Delayed decisions.

- Unexplained no's.

- Escalations that go nowhere.

Cognitive Counter-Move:

16

Reframe the threat as empowerment:

- "This doesn't replace your work—it eliminates the soul-draining parts."

- "It frees you to focus on decisions, not data-wrangling."

- "It makes you look like the most prepared person in the room."

Section 10: The True Goal—Demoing with Empathy, Not Just Excellence

A great cognitive demo is not about showing everything your product can do. It's about showing what your audience's brain can handle, absorb, and believe, within the span of one conversation.

To get there, you must:

- Understand their biases.

- Respect their mental models.

- Bridge to prior knowledge.

- Disarm fear.

- Trigger relevance.

- Tell stories.

In short, become a cognitive guide, not just a software presenter.

Key Takeaways

- Your prospect's brain is preloaded with biases and expectations.
- Mental models, prior knowledge, and stress shape how demos are interpreted.

- Start with relevance and emotional safety.
- Use cognitive science to demo *with* the brain, not against it.

Chapter 2: Cognitive Load – The Silent Killer

How to reduce mental strain so your message gets through.

Section 1: What Is Cognitive Load—and Why Should Salespeople Care?

Imagine you're watching a software demo. The presenter is moving quickly between tabs, describing advanced features, throwing in acronyms, and clicking at a rapid-fire pace. Before long, you're not learning—you're just surviving. You're trying to remember what was just said, figure out where to look on the screen, and still mentally link it to your own work life. This moment? That's cognitive load in action.

Cognitive load refers to the total mental effort used in your working memory. It's a foundational concept in cognitive psychology and instructional design, and it has profound implications for sales presentations, especially software demos, which require real-time learning, comprehension, and decision-making.

Cognitive Load Theory, developed by John Sweller, divides load into three types:

- Intrinsic Load – The inherent difficulty of the material itself. For example, setting up user permissions in enterprise software is intrinsically more complex than clicking "Create New Record."

- Extraneous Load – The unnecessary burden caused by poor delivery, bad visuals, disorganized sequencing, or confusing language. This is where most demos go wrong.

- Germane Load – The productive mental effort used to make sense of what's being presented. This is the kind of load we *want* to increase.

In a sales demo, your goal is to minimize extraneous and manage intrinsic so that there's mental space left for germane. Because here's the truth: if your buyer's brain is full of clutter or confusion, it doesn't matter how great your product is—they won't retain it, they won't trust it, and they certainly won't buy it.

Demos that ignore cognitive load are essentially leaking value. They overwhelm instead of persuade. But once you understand this principle, you can transform every screen share into a clear, focused, and compelling learning experience.

Section 2: Why Software Demos Are Especially Vulnerable

Cognitive overload can occur in any kind of presentation, but software demos are uniquely susceptible. Why? Because they're often live, unscripted, fast-paced, and layered with complexity. Unlike a well-designed slide deck, a software demo requires your audience to interpret what they're seeing and hearing simultaneously, while also trying to map it onto their own mental model of work.

Let's break down why demos carry a higher cognitive load than most forms of business communication:

1. Simultaneous Inputs

In a typical demo, the viewer is listening to the presenter and watching a screen. That sounds simple—but the human brain isn't great at doing both at once, especially when the visual is unfamiliar. If your voice is explaining a function while your mouse darts across a feature-heavy dashboard, your prospect's brain is forced to split its attention, which dramatically reduces retention.

2. Rapid Context Switching

One minute you're in the reporting dashboard, the next in an admin setup screen, then flipping to user management. These shifts might feel natural to you—but for a first-time viewer, it's like flipping between three different apps. Context switching imposes a toll, and the more often you do it without transition or framing, the harder it is for the brain to keep up.

3. High Density of Novelty

Sales demos introduce new terminology, new layouts, new workflows, and new logic structures. The more *novel* the content, the higher the intrinsic load. That means prospects must mentally decode your software *before* they can even start thinking about how it benefits them. If you don't ease that learning curve, their mental capacity gets drained on decoding rather than evaluating.

4. Emotional and Social Pressure

Most demos happen on video calls, often in front of other stakeholders. Prospects may be worried about looking uninformed, reluctant to ask questions, or preoccupied with how they'll explain this solution to their team later. That background anxiety burns cognitive resources, too, and it makes people less likely to admit confusion.

In short, a sales demo isn't just about what you show; it's about what the buyer's brain is capable of processing in that moment. You are not performing for a neutral observer; you are teaching a stressed learner. And if your delivery isn't designed for that mental reality, even your best features will fall flat.

The good news? Most sellers don't know this. Which means you can stand out by designing your demos not just for features, but for cognitive flow.

Section 3: Symptoms of Overload in a Demo

Even the best sales professionals sometimes miss the moment when a demo goes sideways—not because of a product failure or a tough question, but because the audience simply checked out. The demo may still be running, the presenter still speaking, and the screen still sharing—but mentally, the buyer is gone.

This is the quiet and dangerous effect of cognitive overload. And if you can't spot it in real time, your deal may stall without warning or explanation.

Here are the most common symptoms:

1. The Glaze-Over Look

You're clicking through your app and explaining a complex process. You glance at your prospect—and their face is blank. No nodding, no reactions, no light behind the eyes. That's not disinterest, it's mental overload. The brain, like a computer, is freezing due to excess processing. This is often the first warning sign.

2. Silence When You Pause for Input

You ask a simple check-in: "Any questions so far?" Silence. You assume they're following along—but in reality, their cognitive resources are so depleted, they don't even know what to ask. They've lost the thread.

Worse still, silence can create a false sense of approval. The presenter believes they're crushing it. The buyer? Lost in thought or trying to catch up to a click path that passed them five screens ago.

3. Early Objections That Don't Add Up

If a buyer interrupts the demo to say, "This looks really complicated," or "This probably won't work for our team," and you know the feature is actually easy or aligned, they may not be rejecting your product. They're rejecting the mental effort of continuing.

Objections in the early stages of a demo often signal cognitive fatigue, not actual misalignment.

4. Multitasking or Disengagement

The cameras go off. Eyes drift. You see them glancing down, typing, or suddenly needing to "check Slack." Multitasking is a classic sign that the prospect's working memory is at capacity and seeking relief. The brain is retreating into lower-effort tasks to reduce its cognitive strain.

5. The Vanishing Follow-Up

You complete the demo, and the buyer says, "Great, this was really interesting, we'll get back to you soon." Then... nothing. This post-demo silence is often not about price or timing. It's because they can't remember why your product mattered. The demo wasn't retained—it was endured.

The Fix: Real-Time Awareness and Adjustment:

Cognitive overload doesn't have to be fatal if you spot it early. Great demo presenters watch their audience as closely as they watch their product interface. They recognize subtle shifts and adjust in the moment:

- Slow down.

- Reframe.

- Recap.

- Ask a simple yes/no question to reengage.

- Pause the flow and summarize: "Let's take a breath here. What stands out so far?"

The goal is not to power through a feature list. The goal is to keep the brain online. Once you learn to spot these symptoms, your demos become more agile, more responsive, and more connected.

Section 4: Reducing Intrinsic Load Without Dumbing It Down

Not all complexity is bad. After all, your software might be solving a truly difficult problem. But how you present that complexity, especially in a first demo, can make or break your audience's ability to understand and appreciate it. This is where intrinsic cognitive load comes into play.

Intrinsic load is the effort required to process the material itself. Some tasks are just naturally more complex, like configuring permissions in a multi-tenant architecture or setting up conditional automation rules. You can't eliminate this complexity entirely, but you can manage how and when it's introduced.

Here's the key: You don't need to show everything in one go.

1. Focus on Core Workflows, Not Comprehensive Coverage

Many presenters fall into the "let me show you everything" trap. They want to prove value, so they race through every tab, feature, and dashboard. But that strategy overloads the buyer.

Instead, ask yourself:

"What 2–3 workflows solve the biggest pain points I uncovered in discovery?"

Start there. Show a clear beginning, middle, and end for each process. Let the user see themselves moving through the task.

For example:

- Instead of showing every report, show one report that helps the CFO make a critical decision.

- Instead of every alert setting, show how one alert prevents a compliance failure.

2. Use Progressive Disclosure

Progressive disclosure is a design principle used in UX and education: don't reveal everything upfront. Unfold complexity in layers. Let the user grasp a simple interface, then zoom into more advanced functions only if needed.

Say things like:

"Let me show you the high-level view first, and then we can explore the details behind it."

This reduces the mental leap required to make sense of your product. It also keeps the buyer from panicking when they see a dense UI.

3. Use Role-Based or Persona-Based Paths

Tailor the demo to how a specific role would use the tool. For instance, show a support manager's day-in-the-life journey through your platform. This keeps the demo anchored to context your prospect already understands—and it helps isolate only the relevant complexity for their role. A persona-led path naturally limits intrinsic load by trimming what's unnecessary for that individual.

4. Clarify What You're Not Showing

When skipping a section of the product, explain why it's not needed today:

"There's a whole automation engine behind this, but I'm keeping that in our next session with your Ops team—so we can stay focused here."

This reduces FOMO (Fear of Missing Out) while reinforcing that your demo is customized, not incomplete.

When you manage intrinsic load well, your product feels elegant, even if it's powerful. The prospect doesn't feel overwhelmed. Instead, they feel smart, in control, and ready to engage.

Section 5: Eliminating Extraneous Load — The Silent Demo Killer

If intrinsic load is about the inherent complexity of your software, then extraneous load is about the unnecessary difficulty introduced by your presentation style. Think of it as friction caused by poor delivery—cluttered visuals, bad pacing, or confusing language. And in many demos, extraneous load is what quietly kills comprehension.

Even if your product is simple, a poorly structured walkthrough can overwhelm the buyer's brain and diminish your message. The good news? Extraneous load is 100% under your control.

1. Declutter Your Demo Environment

This is the most obvious, and most overlooked, source of extraneous load. An interface crammed with test records, unfinished configurations, or uncollapsed menus creates mental noise. Your buyer doesn't know what's important, where to focus, or how to interpret what they're seeing.

Checklist before sharing your screen:

- Use a clean sandbox or demo account with only relevant, realistic data.

- Collapse any irrelevant sidebars or menus.

- Label tabs or screens in a way that mirrors your buyer's world (e.g., "Client Review" instead of "Form_Layout_04").

- Remove fake or internal labels like "Test User 123" or "BetaPanel v3."

2. Align Your Voice and Visuals

When your voice says one thing, and your mouse shows another, the brain short-circuits. This is known as split attention, and it's one of the most common causes of demo confusion.

Avoid narrating a feature while clicking somewhere else. Instead:

- Speak, then show.

- Use clear verbal anchors: "Watch the top right corner here..."

- Move your mouse deliberately, don't swirl or dart.

Your cursor should act like a spotlight, guiding visual attention in sync with your words.

3. Eliminate Jargon and Insider Terms

You know what API triggers, audit logs, or "synchronous flows" are. Your buyer may not. Every unfamiliar word adds friction. That's extraneous load.

Try this:

- Swap "asynchronous escalation rule" with "a rule that notifies the right person even if they're offline."

- Replace "multi-instance object" with "a group of related entries you can reuse."

Use simple, concrete language whenever possible. Save technical depth for later stages.

4. Slow Your Pace. Then Slow It Again.

Most presenters go 20% too fast. When you know the product inside and out, you forget how long it takes a new viewer to mentally catch up. Every extra click or sentence is another cognitive leap your buyer has to make.

Build in micro-pauses. After a key action, stop talking. Let it sink in. Use phrases like:

"Let me pause here so you can absorb what just happened."

"I'll give you a second to look at this layout—notice how the data is structured."

These intentional silences reduce cognitive strain and increase clarity.

5. Provide Visual and Verbal Wayfinding

Your demo is a journey. If your buyer doesn't know where they are, they'll feel lost. Use signposts along the way:

- "Next, I'll show how this gets approved."

- "This is step two of the intake process."

- "Now we're switching roles—from the manager's view to the auditor's."

This keeps the brain oriented and reduces the load of mentally stitching the pieces together afterward.

Eliminating extraneous load doesn't require changing your product, it just requires changing how you present it. And the result? Your software feels easier, smarter, and more valuable—without changing a single feature.

Section 6: Boosting Germane Load — Helping the Brain Make Meaning

So far, we've discussed how to minimize intrinsic and extraneous cognitive load to prevent overwhelm. But now we shift focus to the third—and most desirable—type: germane load.

Germane load is the mental effort that leads to deep understanding, memory formation, and ultimately, belief. It's the productive type of mental work—the kind that turns passive viewers into engaged buyers. If extraneous load is a leak in your demo, germane load is the engine that drives it forward.

The goal of every sales demo should be to maximize germane load without overloading the brain. This section focuses on how to guide the buyer toward meaning-making, insight, and internalization. This turns attention into understanding, and understanding into belief.

1. Use Analogies and Comparisons

Analogies are shortcuts to understanding. When you compare a complex or novel feature to something familiar, the brain connects the dots faster and with less effort.

Examples:

- "Think of this automation like a self-driving checklist."

- "This module is your digital filing cabinet—but it also alerts you if something's missing."

- "If you've used QuickBooks, this works like their journal entries, but across teams."

The analogy becomes a bridge from the known to the unknown.

2. Stimulate Mental Simulation

The human brain is a simulation engine. When you say, "Imagine you're onboarding a new employee," or "Picture your team submitting a request on Friday afternoon," you activate neural pathways that increase attention, empathy, and memory retention.

Tactics:

- Ask scenario-based questions: "What would it save you if you could run this report daily instead of monthly?"

- Use second-person language: "Here's where *you* would review incoming tasks."

- Invite role-based projection: "This is what your VP of Ops would see when they log in."

This creates personal relevance, and relevance is the fuel for memory.

3. Tell Micro-Stories

Stories are among the most brain-compatible ways to transfer information. Even a 20-second customer anecdote can crystallize a benefit far more powerfully than a feature explanation.

Instead of:

"You can configure approval paths here."

Try:

"A client in manufacturing used this to reduce a five-day approval cycle to just six hours—because the manager could approve directly on their phone during a site visit."

Stories engage the emotional and visual centers of the brain. They don't just explain—they transport.

4. Recap and Reinforce

Germane load works best with repetition. But not redundant repetition—purposeful reinforcement.

Use simple summary phrases:

- "So just to recap: in three clicks, we've created, routed, and tagged this case—something that used to require three separate tools."

- "That whole sequence? That's now automated end-to-end."

- "Let's step back and look at what we just accomplished."

Section 7: Managing Load for Different Personas

It's a mistake to assume everyone in your audience is processing your demo the same way. Different stakeholders have different roles, priorities, attention spans, and decision criteria, and therefore carry different cognitive loads. If you deliver a one-size-fits-all presentation, you risk overloading some and under-engaging others.

Think of your demo as a group hike. The executive wants to see the mountaintop. The daily user wants to know where the trail forks. IT wants to inspect the ropes and bolts on the cliffside. If you don't address their perspectives intentionally, someone will get left behind.

Let's examine how to manage load for the most common buyer personas.

1. Executives: Abstract Thinkers, Low Tolerance for Detail

Cognitive Profile:
Executives have limited time and high cognitive filtering. They're constantly scanning for signals of impact, risk, and ROI. They think in terms of outcomes, not inputs.

How to Manage Load:

- Keep it high-level. Focus on strategic impact, business transformation, and time-to-value.

- Don't bury them in clicks. One powerful workflow is enough—as long as it shows scale or competitive edge.

- Frame everything in their language: "This eliminates $120k in labor hours per year," or "This reduces audit exposure by 80%."

Avoid technical deep dives. The moment they feel lost in the weeds, they mentally check out.

2. Power Users and Team Leads: Operational Thinkers, Detail-Oriented

Cognitive Profile:
These are your doers. They evaluate software based on usability, task alignment, and efficiency. They care deeply about how the tool fits their daily workflow and how much autonomy they'll retain.

How to Manage Load:

- Give them depth, but one workflow at a time.

- Let them visualize *how* they'd use it: "You start your day on this dashboard, which shows your top 5 action items."

- Validate familiarity: "This replaces the Excel tracker you're using now, but it auto-calculates everything."

They appreciate clarity and empowerment. Don't gloss over the day-to-day just to impress the C-suite.

3. IT and Admins: Skeptical Thinkers, Logic-Driven

Cognitive Profile:
IT teams process demos looking for security risks, integration points, and configuration flexibility. They're less interested in the user interface and more interested in what's under the hood.

How to Manage Load:

- Offer brief, structured technical depth, but separate it from the main user flow.

- Say: "Here's the API layer—it integrates with your SSO and supports SCIM provisioning. I'll send the schema after the call."

- Avoid hand-waving. Vagueness increases their cognitive strain and resistance.

These personas often hold veto power. Their load increases when they can't validate your claims.

4. Mixed Audiences: Shared Attention, Conflicting Priorities

Cognitive Profile:
The most cognitively difficult scenario is a mixed room—CFO, manager, IT lead, and end user—all watching the same demo.

Each brings a different filter. Trying to impress everyone at once increases extraneous load for all.

How to Manage Load:

- Use persona signposting: "From a finance view, here's what this means. For operations, notice how fast the turnaround is."

- Segment your demo into mini-blocks. Each one should clearly serve a particular role.

- Invite direct participation: "Let's take a moment—[User Name], does this flow align with how you process requests today?"

Your job isn't to balance evenly—it's to speak directly and briefly to each brain in the room.

Managing load by persona transforms your demo from a generic tour into a tailored conversation. And when each stakeholder feels seen, understood, and empowered—you create consensus, not confusion.

Section 8: The Science Behind Memory and Overload

One of the most frustrating realities in sales is this: you deliver what feels like a solid demo, and yet days later, the prospect can't remember half of what you showed. You left the call confident. But now they're ghosting. What happened?

The answer lies in the mechanics of human memory, and how easily it becomes overwhelmed.

Let's break it down.

Working Memory: The Brain's Holding Tank

Working memory is like a mental whiteboard. It holds temporary information while the brain figures out what to do with it. But here's the catch: it's incredibly limited.

Most studies suggest working memory can hold 4 to 7 discrete chunks of information at one time. Not pages. Not paragraphs. Chunks.

So when you deliver a 30-minute firehose of features—across modules, screens, and roles—you're shoving 50+ chunks into a 7-slot processor. No wonder things slip through the cracks.

And once working memory is full, new information replaces old—unless that info is:

1. Reinforced,

2. Emotionally charged, or

3. Connected to something familiar.

If it isn't? It's gone.

Long-Term Memory: The Real Goal of Your Demo

Selling doesn't happen during the call. It happens after—when your champion talks to their boss, revisits their notes, or recalls your value prop during procurement discussions.

That means your most important demo content must reach long-term memory—the part of the brain that stores retrievable meaning.

To make that leap, your message must:

- Be relevant and personal

- Be logically structured

- Be emotionally or visually memorable

- Be repeated or reinforced

This is where most demos fail. They exceed working memory and never give key ideas a chance to transfer.

Chunking: A Core Tactic for Memory-Based Demos

Chunking is the process of grouping related information together so it's stored as *one* unit rather than several. For example:

- "Create, route, and approve a case" = 3 steps → 1 meaningful chunk: *automated workflow*

- "Dashboard, alerts, and actions" = 3 tabs → 1 chunk: *real-time visibility*

Chunked content reduces working memory strain and makes retention more likely.

Try organizing your demo into:

- 3 workflows

- 3 user roles

- 3 pain points addressed

Why three? Because the Rule of Threes matches how working memory naturally handles patterns.

Cognitive Overload = Memory Abandonment

The scientific truth is simple: once working memory is full, the brain starts dumping content. It doesn't do this with conscious permission—it happens automatically to protect the system from overheating.

You might think your 12-tab tour was comprehensive. But what your buyer remembers is:

- The confusing part with the nested menus,

- The phrase you repeated three times,

- And the one feature that sparked a story or emotion.

Everything else? Evaporated.

Demo for Memory, Not Just Accuracy

Your goal isn't to show *everything*. It's to show what the brain can:

- Grasp in the moment,

- Rehearse during the call, and

- Recall after the meeting.

To get there, build in intentional repetition, chunk key ideas, and use language designed to stick:

"This is the big win—this replaces three of your manual workflows." "I'm going to say that again because it's important..." "This is the part our clients say they *can't live without*."

That's memory design. And it's your secret weapon.

Section 9: Prepping for Load-Managed Demos

Most salespeople prep for demos by building feature lists, checking environments, and rehearsing transitions. These are important. But if you want to deliver a cognitively effective demo—one that matches how the brain learns—you need a new kind of preparation: load management planning.

That means designing a demo experience that protects the buyer's working memory, eliminates confusion, and guides them toward meaningful insight.

Here's how to do it.

1. Identify Your 2–3 Core Messages

If your prospect remembers only three things tomorrow, what should they be?

Before you open your demo environment, write down:

- The one workflow that demonstrates immediate value

- The one feature that differentiates you

- The one outcome that aligns with their business goal

Everything else supports those pillars. Anything that distracts from them adds unnecessary load.

Example:

"Today I want you to walk away knowing: how we cut manual intake time in half, how you can automate case routing, and how your finance team gains real-time visibility into approvals."

That framing narrows their mental scope—making your message easier to remember.

2. Clean Your Demo Environment Ruthlessly

Cognitive overload often begins before you even speak—because your screen is too busy. Too many buttons, too much data, too many irrelevant labels.

Before every demo:

- Clear out dummy records or rename them to reflect your prospect's world.

- Remove sidebars, test menus, and unnecessary modules.

- Use minimal, high-impact data—realistic enough to be relatable, but not cluttered.

- Consider using visual placeholders like "CEO Dashboard" or "Approval Queue" instead of default terminology.

This makes the interface look easier to understand, which primes the brain for better processing.

3. Script Signposts and Recaps

You don't need a word-for-word script—but you do need intentional phrasing that reduces cognitive strain.

Plan to insert:

- Signposts: "Here's where we start... Now we move to the team view... This is the final approval screen."

- Recaps: "So just to summarize: we created a record, tagged it for review, and auto-notified the team."

- Framing language: "This next part may look complex, but it's actually just two clicks."

These moments act as memory anchors. They help the brain build a mental map of your product.

4. Customize Based on Persona Load

Are you demoing to a CFO or an operations manager? An engineer or a legal analyst?

Load management is about cognitive empathy:

- For execs: cut complexity, emphasize impact.

- For users: focus on speed and simplicity.

- For IT: deliver clarity, not just technical depth.

Write down one key phrase or question tailored to each persona before the call. This helps you speak their mental language during the live moment.

5. Prepare for Load Recovery Moments

Even the best demos encounter hiccups—bugs, distractions, fatigue. Build in moments to reset cognitive overload.

Have a few "load relief" lines ready:

"Let's pause there—what stands out so far?"

"I'm going to rewind and do that one more time slowly."

"That was a lot at once—would it help to see that in a quick summary view?"

These statements reduce pressure and give the buyer space to mentally catch up—without losing confidence in you or your product.

When you prep a demo through the lens of cognitive design, you're not just showing a product—you're crafting a *learning experience*. And when the brain feels safe, focused, and in control, belief becomes possible.

Section 10: Cognitive Load as a Competitive Advantage

Most software sellers are focused on product superiority, pricing strategy, or feature differentiation. These are all valid points of competition. But in today's crowded marketplace, they're not always enough.

What if the real edge, the invisible advantage, was not in what you sell, but in how you present it? Understanding and managing cognitive load gives you that edge.

Because when buyers are confused, they don't ask clarifying questions—they walk away. When they're overwhelmed, they don't remember features; they forget you. When they're emotionally taxed, they don't say "Yes"—they delay. But when they're mentally engaged, emotionally at ease, and guided through a clear and meaningful flow, they move forward.

Cognitive Simplicity = Perceived Product Simplicity

It doesn't matter how intuitive your software actually is—perception is everything. If your demo feels complex, your product feels complex. If your message is disorganized, your solution feels disorganized.

On the flip side, a clear, structured, calm demo experience leads the buyer to think:

"This is going to be easy to roll out."

"My team won't resist this."

"We can hit the ground running."

And that's before they've even touched the tool themselves.

The product didn't change; you did. Your clarity became their confidence.

You Are Competing Against Mental Fatigue:

In most sales cycles, your demo is one of several the buyer is watching that week. Some are better funded. Some are more well-known. But almost all of them are mentally taxing.

That means the winning demo isn't necessarily the flashiest—it's the one the buyer remembers, understands, and feels good about afterward.

Managing cognitive load means:

- They walk away remembering what made your product unique.

- They're not embarrassed to retell your story to internal stakeholders.

- They feel empowered, not exhausted.

In other words, you make them look and feel smart, and people love to say yes to that.

Scalability Through Cognitive Design

Cognitive demo design isn't just about performance—it's about process. Once your team understands these principles, they become a framework that scales:

- Use the same chunked narrative structure across teams.

- Embed signposting and role-based messaging in training.

- Evaluate demo recordings not just on content, but on cognitive clarity.

The payoff? Higher demo conversion rates. Shorter sales cycles. Fewer ghosted follow-ups. And a team that sells with psychological precision, not just product knowledge.

The Demo Isn't Just a Pitch—It's a Cognitive Experience

Once you start seeing your demo through the lens of the brain, everything changes:

- Every feature has a learning curve.

- Every slide has a memory limit.

- Every moment of silence has strategic value.

And when you respect that reality, your demos move from routine to resonant.

Final Summary: Chapter 2 Takeaways

- Cognitive load is the most underestimated cause of demo failure.
- Software demos are especially vulnerable due to novelty, multitasking, and complexity.
- Managing intrinsic, extraneous, and germane load turns demos into effective learning experiences.
- Tailoring load by persona and prepping with intention gives every demo a better chance to succeed.
- Mastering cognitive load is not just a tactic—it's a strategic, scalable sales advantage.

Chapter 4: Emotion in Demo Retention

Why feelings fuel memory—and how to use emotion as a strategic lever in software demos.

Section 1: Why Emotion Enhances Memory

The science behind why feelings stick longer than facts.

When people think about improving demos, they usually focus on clarity, product knowledge, and smooth navigation. But the most overlooked, and most powerful tool in your demo is emotion.

That's not just a sales cliché. It's neuroscience.

Emotionally charged moments are more likely to be remembered because they activate the amygdala, a part of the brain that plays a key role in processing emotions and flagging important memories. When the amygdala is engaged, it sends a signal to the hippocampus—essentially telling it: "Store this. It matters."

This mechanism is why you can remember where you were during a major life event—but forget what was on yesterday's to-do list. Emotion gives memory weight.

In a sales context, this means that the buyer is far more likely to remember:

The moment you showed how your platform removes a pain they hate.

The story about a client in their shoes who succeeded.

- The way you framed a metric that ties directly to their job stress.

What they're less likely to remember? The fourth setting in your configuration menu. Emotion enhances retention. But it also enhances meaning. It helps the brain decide what to care about, what to focus on, and what to share with others.

Importantly, this isn't about theatrics. You don't need to be dramatic or manipulative. Emotional engagement in demos isn't about making people feel overwhelmed—it's about making them feel seen, understood, and hopeful.

In the next section, we'll explore why emotion is already in the room—even in buttoned-up business settings—and how to spot and respond to it.

Section 2: Emotion in a Business Context — It's Already There

Why every buyer brings more than logic into your demo.

There's a common myth in B2B sales that business decisions are made purely on logic, numbers, and rational evaluation. But beneath the spreadsheets and decision matrices, emotion is always present—even if it's subtle or unspoken.

Your buyer doesn't walk into a demo as a blank slate. They bring with them a cocktail of workplace stress, internal politics, job security concerns, professional pride, and past frustrations with other tools. Every one of these factors colors how they experience your presentation.

Here are a few examples of the kinds of emotion already in the room:

A manager who's exhausted by broken workflows is hoping for relief.

- A director who championed a failed rollout last year is feeling nervous.

- An operations lead who's tired of being ignored is seeking validation.
- An executive under pressure to cut costs is quietly feeling urgency.

Even if these emotions aren't voiced, they influence everything: how closely your buyer pays attention, how quickly they make connections, how they interpret your tone—and whether they walk away excited or indifferent.

Smart demo presenters don't ignore this. They read the emotional context and shape their delivery to meet it. That could mean starting slower, asking more reflective questions, or pausing to validate the buyer's current state before showing off a solution.

Remember: every demo is both a technical walkthrough and an emotional negotiation. If you miss the second, the first often won't matter.

In the next section, we'll explore the typical emotional arc of a demo—and how you can intentionally guide it from skepticism to confidence.

Section 3: The Emotional Arc of a Demo

From tension to trust—how your buyer's feelings evolve during the call.

Every demo has a hidden emotional journey. Even if your buyer never cracks a smile or frowns, their internal state is constantly shifting. Recognizing this arc—and designing for it—can be the difference between a forgettable walkthrough and a resonant, persuasive experience. Most buyers go through three emotional phases during a demo:

1. The Opening: Skepticism, Stress, or Distraction
At the start, your buyer may be mentally scattered. They're worried about other meetings. They might be skeptical of another sales pitch. Or they've had a bad experience with software rollouts in the past. This is where your job is to lower defenses. Use empathy, clarity, and quick wins to create safety and curiosity.

Examples:

"We'll keep this simple and focused on your team's biggest challenge."

"I'll show you just what's relevant for your workflow—nothing extra."

2. The Middle: Engagement and Curiosity
Once you establish relevance and reduce anxiety, the buyer leans in. They start asking questions. They picture how this applies to their world. This is your moment to guide their attention and build excitement through clear outcomes, relatable stories, and role-specific impact.

3. The Close: Relief, Hope, or Momentum

If the demo has gone well, the buyer feels something subtle but powerful: relief. Relief that the solution is simpler than they feared. Relief that it could work. Hope that they won't be stuck with their current problem forever. This is when belief starts to form—and when action becomes possible.

In the next section, we'll examine how to deliberately trigger and reinforce key emotions throughout your demo to deepen memory and impact.

Section 4: Emotional Triggers That Reinforce Key Moments

Strategically building emotional resonance into your demo flow.

Emotion isn't just a byproduct of a good demo—it can be a deliberate design element. Certain emotional "spikes" help the brain decide what to remember, what to share, and what to believe. As a presenter, you can structure your demo to include these emotional triggers at the right moments.

Let's look at a few powerful emotional levers and how to use them:

Relief: Solving What Feels Broken

Buyers are often burdened by manual work, complex processes, or endless spreadsheets. When you show how your software eliminates one of those pain points, you're offering relief, and that moment becomes a turning point in the demo.

Example:

"Remember that five-step handoff you mentioned? Here it happens in one click—automatically."

The sigh, the nod, the slight smile—those are signs of emotional relief, and they're strong memory anchors.

Empowerment: Giving Back Control

Demos that make the buyer feel more capable and independent trigger pride and excitement. Show how your platform gives non-technical users the power to do things they'd normally outsource.

Example:

"You don't need to wait on IT—this form builder lets you launch updates yourself in seconds."

Recognition: Feeling Understood

If you describe a pain point in their words before they do, you create instant connection. Recognition creates trust.

Example:

"We hear from a lot of teams that version control is a nightmare. That's why every edit here is auto-tracked."

In the next section, we'll explore how your tone, phrasing, and framing can amplify or suppress these emotional moments—often more than the feature itself.

Section 5: Tone, Voice, and Framing Matter More Than Features
How you say it shapes how they feel about what you show.

In a demo, features are only part of the story. Two presenters can show the exact same workflow, but one leaves the buyer inspired, while the other leaves them cold. The difference? Tone, voice, and framing.
Your tone isn't just about being friendly or professional. It's about emotional resonance—the way your delivery either amplifies clarity and confidence or fuels confusion and doubt.

Tone Signals Trust:
A calm, confident tone tells the buyer, "This is under control." If you rush, sound uncertain, or talk like you're reading from a manual, the buyer senses it, and their anxiety increases. But if your voice is warm, steady, and human, it lowers resistance and invites attention.

Try this:

"Let me show you something our clients love..."

Instead of:

"Next I'm going to demonstrate the forms module."

Framing Shapes Perception:

Framing is how you position a feature before or after you show it. A generic setup—"Here's a settings page"—adds no value. But if you say:

"This is where you customize escalation paths—so your team never misses an urgent case..."

Suddenly, it has purpose. It solves something. It matters.

Language Builds or Breaks Emotional Walls

Avoid passive phrases like:

- "You might be able to..."
- "It kind of works like..."

Instead, use empowering, declarative statements:

- "This replaces your manual task tracker."

- "This dashboard shows exactly what needs your attention every morning."

Your voice is more than narration—it's the emotional container for your message. In the next section, we'll explore how storytelling can deepen that connection even further.

Section 6: Using Storytelling to Drive Emotional Engagement
Turning features into feelings through short, impactful narratives.

Nothing activates the human brain like a story. Neuroscience shows that storytelling doesn't just engage more areas of the brain—it also triggers empathy, improves retention, and creates emotional resonance. That makes it one of the most powerful tools in your demo toolkit. Why? Because stories transport your buyer. Instead of watching a feature, they experience its impact. Instead of interpreting abstract data, they relate to a human outcome. And when that happens, emotion—and memory—lock in.

The Simple Story Structure for Demos
You don't need a novel. A 20-second story can shift the energy in the room. Try this format:

1. Problem: Briefly describe a challenge a real client faced.
2. Tension: What made it difficult, urgent, or costly?
3. Resolution: How your product solved it—and what happened next.

Example:

"A healthcare group we worked with had intake requests sitting in email for days. One manager told us, 'I don't even know what's been missed.' We set up this dashboard view—and in less than a week, they cut processing time by 40%." That's not just a workflow, it's a win.

Tips for Effective Storytelling in Demos:

- Use industry-specific examples when possible.
- Keep it short—1–3 sentences max.
- Use real quotes or paraphrased language for authenticity.
- Tie the resolution to something the buyer cares about: time, clarity, control.

Stories don't just explain, they connect. They turn your software from a set of functions into a tool for transformation.

In the next section, we'll explore how surprise and delight—small moments of emotional spike—can become the highlights buyers remember and repeat.

Section 7: Using Surprise and Delight to Create Demo Highlights

Small moments that make a big emotional—and memorable— impact.

The most talked-about part of your demo may not be a major feature or complex workflow. It might be a small moment that sparks an unexpected reaction: "Wait—did that just happen automatically?" That flash of surprise, that sudden sense of delight, can leave a lasting impression. Surprise and delight are powerful because they trigger an emotional spike. The brain flags it as important and stores it for later. It's a technique used in great storytelling, customer service, and yes, software demos.

What Surprise and Delight Looks Like in a Demo:
These moments don't need to be flashy or dramatic. They just need to deliver more ease, clarity, or value than the buyer expected. Examples:

- A button auto-generates a fully formatted report with one click.
- A change in one field instantly updates downstream approvals.
- A clean, role-specific dashboard replaces multiple spreadsheets.

What makes it surprising is not just the action—but the contrast to how hard it used to be.

How to Deliver These Moments Effectively

1. Pause and Let It Land

   Don't rush past it. Say:

"Watch this next part—this is where it gets fun."

Then let the result speak for itself.

2. Use Buyer-Centered Framing

"This usually takes your team 45 minutes, right? Now it's one click."

3. Watch for Reactions and Build On Them

   If someone smiles, laughs, or nods—lean into it. Say:

"Exactly—that's what we love hearing."

These micro-moments create demo highlights—the parts your buyer tells others about. In the next section, we'll focus on how to spot and adapt to emotional signals during the demo itself.

Section 8: Reading the Room – Emotional Intelligence in Live Demos

Recognizing unspoken signals and adapting in real time.

A great demo isn't just about what you say—it's about what you sense. Emotional intelligence is the skill that lets you read subtle cues, adjust your pacing, and respond to how your buyer is *feeling*, not just what they're saying.

Even in virtual meetings, the room speaks—through body language, tone, silence, or quick shifts in energy. Tuning into these signals helps you deliver a more connected and persuasive presentation.

What to Watch For:
- Facial expressions: Raised eyebrows, head tilts, frowns, or sudden smiles are signals of confusion, curiosity, or delight.
- Body language: Leaning in = interest. Leaning back or crossing arms = possible skepticism.
- Verbal cues: "Hmm..." or "Interesting..." may mean curiosity—or quiet concern.
- Silence: Sometimes silence means engagement; other times, it's confusion or overload. Trust your gut—but verify with gentle check-ins.

How to Adjust in Real Time
- If you sense disengagement, pause and invite interaction:
"Would it help to see that flow one more time?"
- If you detect excitement, don't brush past it:
"That reaction makes me think this hits home. Want to go deeper?"
- If a moment lands flat, reframe it:
"That came out a bit dry—let me show you what it really does for your team."

The most successful presenters aren't just good speakers—they're excellent listeners. They make the buyer feel seen and safe, which creates space for trust, emotion, and momentum.

Next, we'll look at how to tailor emotional resonance by persona—because a CFO and a frontline user don't react to the same story.

Section 9: Aligning Emotion to Role and Persona

Not every buyer feels the same pain—or the same excitement.

Emotional resonance isn't one-size-fits-all. A feature that excites a frontline user might worry a CTO. A story that moves an operations lead might sound irrelevant to a CFO. That's why emotional design in your demo must be tailored to persona.

Each role in the room brings different pressures, goals, and cognitive filters. If you want your demo to connect deeply, you must speak to the emotional landscape of each stakeholder.

Executives: Emotion = Confidence and Control
What they want:

- Strategic clarity
- Reduced risk
- Predictable impact

What resonates:

- Phrases like "real-time visibility," "audit-proof," or "aligned to KPIs"
- Screens that simplify dashboards, forecasts, or compliance reporting
- Emotional triggers: confidence, clarity, decisiveness

Avoid: Deep feature dives. They overload execs and reduce perceived value.

Users and Managers: Emotion = Ease and Relief

What they want:
- Simpler workflows
- Fewer mistakes
- Less frustration

What resonates:
- Click paths that cut steps
- Automation that replaces routine work
- Emotional triggers: relief, validation, empowerment

Phrase it as:

"This saves your team an hour a day—and removes the manual chase."

IT and Admins: Emotion = Trust and Stability

What they want:
- Integration
- Security

- Autonomy

What resonates:

- Architecture diagrams
- Admin controls
- Emotional triggers: trust, control, certainty

Use calm, confident language:

"Everything you saw today runs within your existing SSO environment."

In our final section, we'll tie it all together—how emotion not only powers memory, but creates forward momentum that carries beyond the demo.

Section 10: From Emotional Connection to Persuasive Momentum

When the feeling survives, so does the sale.

You've delivered a demo that made the buyer feel something— relief, excitement, understanding, or trust. Now what?

The job isn't done. In fact, this is the part most sellers overlook: emotion doesn't just create a better experience—it creates momentum. When your demo connects emotionally, it gives your buyer the energy and clarity to take the next step—and to carry your message forward to others.

Retelling Emotion Fuels:

Most deals don't get closed in the demo—they get closed in internal conversations afterward. When your champion recaps the experience to their team or boss, they're not sharing your script— they're sharing how the demo made them *feel*.

Examples:

"It actually looked easy."

"I could see us using this right away."

"They really understood what we're dealing with."

These are emotional impressions. And they're often the tipping point in buy-in.

Emotion Anchors Memory and Action:

A buyer who feels confident is more likely to act. A buyer who feels uncertain will stall. Emotion is what turns knowledge into belief, and belief into behavior.

This is why demos that lack emotional tone, however accurate, often fade. The brain stores what it cares about. And caring comes from feeling.

The Emotional Checklist for Every Demo:

Before you go live, ask:

- Where will they feel relief?
- Where will they feel empowered?

- Where will they feel seen?

If you can answer those three, you're not just demoing. You're moving people.

In the next chapter, we'll explore how to structure your demo timeline around the brain's memory curve, ensuring that key moments are timed and spaced for maximum retention.

Chapter 3: Working vs. Long-Term Memory

Designing demos that don't just capture attention, but create lasting recall and buying momentum.

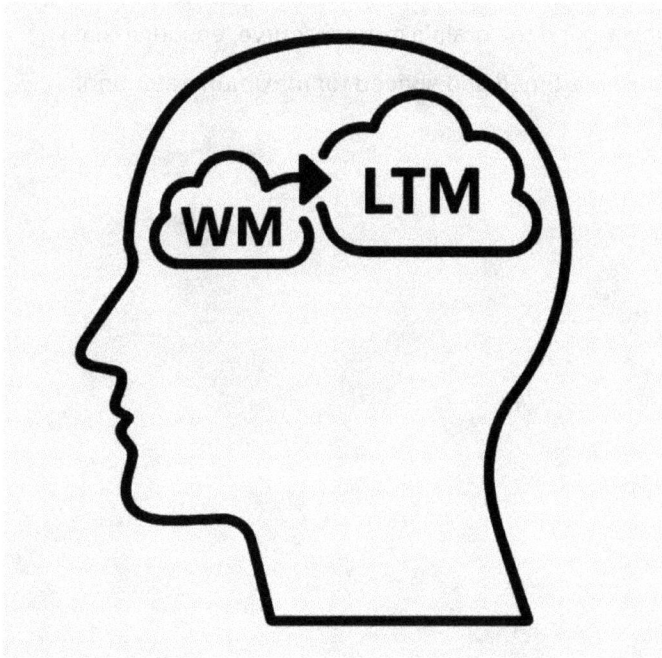

Section 1: The Brain's Two Memory Systems

Understanding how attention becomes belief—or fades away.

Sales presentations, especially software demos, live and die in the space between two systems of memory: working memory and long-term memory. And most fail because they never make the leap from the first to the second.

Working memory is the brain's temporary workspace. It's where your audience holds and juggles bits of information as they try to make sense of what you're showing. But it has strict limitations. Research suggests working memory can only handle 4 to 7 chunks of information at once, and only for a short time, typically seconds to minutes.

In contrast, long-term memory is where knowledge becomes durable. It's where your product's value needs to end up if you want the buyer to recall and advocate for it next week. Long-term memory isn't just for facts—it stores meaning. It's the foundation of confidence, internal alignment, and decision-making.

Here's the challenge: most demos overload working memory with too many screens, too much detail, or disconnected messaging. And when working memory fills up, the brain starts dumping data to make room. If your message isn't reinforced, emotionally engaging, or structured to support memory transfer, it simply vanishes.

Your job in a demo is not just to explain. It's to bridge the gap between temporary understanding and lasting belief. That means intentionally designing for memory—using stories, anchors, structure, and repetition to guide what sticks and what fades. In the next section, we'll explore just how quickly that forgetting happens—and why most demos are forgotten within hours.

Section 2: The Fate of Most Demos — Forgotten Within Hours

Why even great demos disappear from memory—and what to do about it.

The harsh truth is this: most demos are forgotten within 24 hours. Not because the product was bad or the presentation weak, but because the brain is designed to forget what it doesn't immediately need.

This phenomenon is explained by the Ebbinghaus Forgetting Curve, a concept from 19th-century psychologist Hermann Ebbinghaus. His research showed that without reinforcement, people forget nearly 70% of new information within one day, and up to 90% within a week. Sales demos, unfortunately, are a perfect match for this memory drop-off.

Here's how it happens:

A buyer watches your demo. They're interested, but they're also checking emails, worrying about a meeting later, or listening with only half their attention. They process your content in the moment using working memory, but there's no structure, story, or emotional resonance to trigger long-term encoding. So as soon as the call ends, competing priorities rush in, and your carefully crafted pitch begins to fade.

What remains? A vague impression. Maybe a feature they liked. A general sense of professionalism. But the real value, such as the logic, benefits, and use cases, just slip away, especially if your competitors follow with similar demos. This isn't a failure of effort; it's a failure of memory design.

If your goal is to influence buying decisions, your demo can't just be informative. It must be memorable. That means presenting fewer ideas, framed more clearly, and supported by cues that help the brain retain what matters.

In the next section, we'll explore what gets remembered and how to use that knowledge to your advantage.

Section 3: What Gets Remembered—and Why

The ingredients of sticky demos.

Not all content is created equal in the brain's eyes. Some moments during your demo will stick like glue. Others will vanish within minutes. Understanding what gets remembered—and why—gives you a tactical advantage in designing high-impact demos. Research in neuroscience and psychology shows that the brain prioritizes memory around meaning, emotion, relevance, and pattern recognition. In sales demos, that translates to a few key elements:

1. Emotionally Charged Moments

If your demo triggers a moment of relief, surprise, or recognition— "That's exactly what we need!"—the emotional spike enhances memory retention. The amygdala flags emotionally important events, increasing the likelihood that they'll be stored long-term.

2. Visually Anchored Content
Visually clean screens, labeled with familiar terms, or showing side-by-side transformations are easier to recall. A graph that shows time savings, or a before-and-after workflow, creates a mental snapshot your buyer can describe later.

3. Stories and Analogies

Stories are memory superchargers. A short anecdote about a similar client achieving results resonates far more than a feature walkthrough. Analogies simplify complexity, making abstract features relatable.

4. Repetition with Framing

Buyers remember what they hear more than once—especially when it's framed as a takeaway. "Here's the big win," or "This is the part our clients rave about," acts as a signal to the brain: store this.

In short, demos are not retained because of volume; they're retained because of designed moments. Your job is to build these memory anchors into your presentation with intention. Next, we'll explore how working memory gets overloaded and how you can avoid losing your audience mid-demo.

Section 4: How Working Memory Gets Overloaded in Real-Time

Why your audience zones out—and what to do about it.

Working memory is a fragile system. It's easily overwhelmed by too much input, and in a live sales demo, that overload happens faster than most presenters realize. Every second of your presentation, your buyer is trying to listen, read, interpret, and imagine how your software applies to their world. That's a lot to manage, and when too much comes at once, the brain starts dropping data to survive. Here's how most demos accidentally overload working memory:

1. Visual and Verbal Mismatch

Talking about one thing while your screen shows another creates "split attention." The brain must toggle between two channels, what you're saying and what's being shown—without a clear link. That division strains capacity and slows processing.

2. Rapid Context Switching

Jumping between tabs, modules, or user roles without transitions forces the brain to reset constantly. This is known as cognitive switching cost, and it's mentally exhausting, especially if the buyer is unfamiliar with your interface.

3. Feature Dumping

Rattling off multiple features in a single breath—"And then you can tag, assign, filter, export, schedule, and notify..."—may feel impressive, but it overwhelms the brain's ability to organize and prioritize information.

4. No Time to Process

When you move from screen to screen without pause or reflection, you deny the brain the space it needs to encode meaning. You're not just losing attention, you're losing retention.

The solution isn't to oversimplify. It's to pace with cognition in mind. Show one idea at a time. Pause. Recap. Then move forward. In the next section, we'll examine how a structured flow can help working memory succeed—and move your message into long-term memory.

Section 5: The Role of Structure in Memory Transfer

How clear sequencing helps information stick.

If working memory is the brain's inbox, structure is what organizes and delivers the contents to long-term storage. Without structure, your demo becomes a scattered blur. With it, your presentation becomes a guided experience, and your message has a much higher chance of being remembered.

Structure doesn't just make your delivery smoother. It gives the buyer's brain a map to follow, allowing them to recognize patterns, link ideas, and reduce mental strain.

Here are the core structural elements that support memory:

1. Clear Openings and Endings

The brain remembers what happens first and last—this is the primacy/recency effect. Open your demo by stating what they'll see and why it matters. End each section with a crisp recap and benefit statement. This bookending creates cognitive boundaries around key ideas.

2. Signposted Transitions

Use verbal cues to help the audience follow your journey:
"Let's switch now to the approval process..."
"Now that we've seen the dashboard, let's dive into reporting."
These signposts reduce the load of figuring out "Where are we?" and allow the brain to track context.

3. Logical Sequencing

Present your content in a way that mirrors the buyer's workflow. Don't jump from admin to analytics to notifications—walk through a day in the life. Sequencing builds familiarity and helps the brain build mental scaffolding.

4. Themed Groupings

Group features into categories: "Here are the three tools that automate your follow-ups..." This makes it easier to chunk information and recall it later as one idea, not six.

In the next section, we'll explore how to embed specific memory anchors that make your message unmissable and unforgettable.

Section 6: Memory Anchors — How to Make Your Message Stick

Creating moments your buyer will remember—and repeat.

In a demo packed with information, only a few moments will survive the forgetting curve. Your goal is to make those moments intentional. That's where memory anchors come in.

A memory anchor is a phrase, visual, or emotional moment that gives the brain something solid to attach meaning to—something it can grab, repeat, and explain later. These anchors are critical for helping your champion retell your story internally, and for making your product memorable beyond the call.
Here are four powerful types of memory anchors you can build into your demo:

1. Branded or Catchy Phrases

Use phrasing that is clear, sticky, and easy to repeat. Examples:

"This is your Monday-morning clarity screen."

"One-click audit trail—so you never miss a red flag again."

"We call this the autopilot for your approvals."
The more conversational and visual the phrase, the more likely it is to survive in memory.

2. Bold Benefit Summaries

End key sections with a punchline:

"So in three clicks, you just replaced four tools and 90 minutes a day."

This anchors the feature in an outcome—and outcomes are what buyers remember.

3. Memorable Visuals

Show transformations, not just interfaces. Side-by-side "before and after" screens or a simplified workflow diagram can become mental snapshots that explain your value in seconds.

4. Relatable Stories

Tell short, specific customer stories that align with your buyer's industry or challenge. A well-placed narrative is often the most powerful anchor of all.

In the next section, we'll explore how spaced repetition inside your demo can further strengthen these anchors.

Section 7: Spaced Repetition Inside the Demo

Reinforcing key ideas without sounding repetitive.

In cognitive psychology, spaced repetition is the principle that information is better retained when it's reviewed at intervals, rather than crammed all at once. The more often the brain encounters an idea—spread over time—the more likely it is to encode it in long-term memory.

This concept is often used in education and language learning, but it's just as powerful in sales demos. Yet most presenters avoid repetition, fearing they'll sound redundant or boring. The truth is: the brain craves well-placed repetition.

1. Why It Works in Demos

Your buyer is juggling distractions—email pings, Slack messages, internal politics, decision fatigue. They're not retaining everything the first time. Repeating key takeaways—subtly and strategically—ensures your message survives their divided attention.

2.   How to Use Spaced Repetition Effectively
Echo Core Ideas Across Features

If your big win is "automated handoffs," repeat it across the demo:

"This same automation engine powers your intake flow, your routing logic, and your compliance alerts."

3.   Use Callbacks

Later in the demo, refer back to an earlier moment:

"Remember when we tagged a case for review? That's what triggers this instant dashboard update."

4.   Frame Repetition as Value

When repeating, highlight *why* it matters:
"I want to say this again because our clients tell us it's a game-changer..."

5.   Close with a Recap

Your final 90 seconds should repeat the 2–3 biggest takeaways, using slightly different words and framing to deepen recall.

In the next section, we'll look at how asking small, well-timed questions can further enhance retention by engaging the brain's decision-making centers.

Section 8: Interactive Memory — Ask to Activate

Using simple questions to deepen engagement and retention.

One of the fastest ways to activate memory is to get the buyer's brain involved. Research shows that people remember more of what they say than what they hear. When you ask questions, especially low-pressure, reflective ones, you shift the buyer from passive viewer to active participant.

This shift does something powerful: it engages multiple areas of the brain. It forces the prospect to retrieve prior knowledge, imagine use cases, and emotionally invest in your solution. All of this supports long-term memory formation.

1.   Use Reflection to Lock In Understanding

Try questions like:

"How would this change your current approval process?"

"What part of this would your team use first?"

"Would this eliminate anything you're doing manually now?"

These aren't trap questions. They're cognitive bridges—connecting your solution to the buyer's world.

2.   Use Role-Based Prompts

Tailor your questions to who's in the room:

For users: "Where does this fit in your current workflow?"

For execs: "Does this align with the KPIs you're tracking?"

For IT: "How would this map to your current system setup?"

Even if they don't answer out loud, the question prompts internal processing, which increases recall.

3.   Keep It Safe and Optional

Avoid cold-calling someone mid-demo. Instead, frame it softly:

"You don't have to answer, but just think—would this solve the bottleneck you mentioned earlier?"

This gives them space to engage without pressure.

In the next section, we'll explore how to continue reinforcing memory after the demo ends, using well-designed follow-up assets and techniques.

Section 9: Designing Follow-Up Touchpoints for Long-Term Memory

Reinforce, remind, and revive—after the demo ends.

Even the best live demo won't fully stick unless it's reinforced after the call. That's not a failure of presentation—it's how memory works. Your buyer is likely watching multiple demos, juggling priorities, and trying to retell what they saw to others. If you don't help shape what they remember, that memory will either fade or be reshaped inaccurately.
This is why great sellers treat the post-demo window as a second opportunity to build memory.

1. The Summary Email That Replays the Story

Go beyond "Thanks for your time." Recap the key takeaways in the same language you used during the call. Reinforce benefits, not just features:

"As we saw today, the system cuts down intake time by 60%, routes tasks automatically, and gives your leadership team real-time reporting."

Bullet points are helpful, but phrase them as outcomes, not checkboxes.

2. The Demo Highlight Reel

If your org supports recorded demos, send a 2–3 minute video recap showing the most memorable screens or workflows. Include brief narration or callouts to reinforce what the buyer saw. A short video is easier to share internally and keeps your message intact when relayed.

3. One-Pagers or Visual Leave-Behinds

Attach a single, well-designed page that summarizes:
The problem you solve
The 2–3 workflows shown
The business value of each
Bonus: Add icons, diagrams, or role-specific language. This acts as a visual memory anchor that can live beyond the inbox.

In the final section of this chapter, we'll connect memory to motion, showing how recall turns into momentum inside the buying process.

Section 10: From Memory to Momentum

Why what they remember is what gets shared—and sold.

You might think your demo's purpose is to convince the buyer in real time. But that's only part of the story. The real test happens after the meeting, when your buyer becomes the storyteller.

They talk to their manager. They pitch your solution in a budget review. They compare you to a competitor they saw yesterday. In those moments, they don't have your screen, your voice, or your slides. All they have is memory.

76

And memory is what drives momentum.

1. Memory = Shareability

When a buyer can clearly remember what you showed—and why it matters—they can confidently share it with others. Your demo becomes replayable. It transforms from a moment in time to a shared internal narrative.
A few key phrases or visual anchors can make the difference:

"It's the tool that cut intake time in half."

"Remember that dashboard with the auto-prioritized cases?"

"They showed a customer just like us who saved 8 hours a week."

2. Momentum Comes from Retellable Stories

Great demos give buyers simple, sticky language to use when advocating for you. If they can't repeat what you said, they can't win support. But if you've embedded memory anchors, emotion, and structure? Now they're not just interested—they're empowered.

3. Your Goal Is Transferable Conviction

You're not just trying to get a "yes" in the room. You're trying to plant conviction that can survive outside the room. When you design your demos for memory, you're not just educating—you're enabling. You equip your champion to champion you.

Next, in Chapter 4, we'll explore the role of emotion in demo retention—and how to use it as an amplifier for memory and motivation.

Chapter 5: The Primacy–Recency Advantage

How to time your key moments around what the brain remembers best.

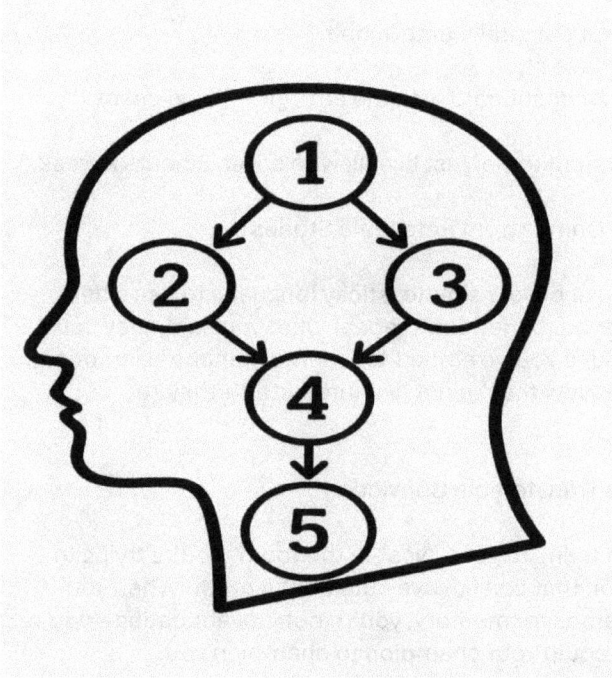

Section 1: The Science Behind Primacy and Recency

What comes first and last gets remembered most.

Have you ever noticed that people often remember the beginning and end of a presentation—but struggle to recall the middle? That's not a fluke. It's a well-documented psychological principle known as the Primacy–Recency Effect.

First introduced by psychologist Hermann Ebbinghaus and confirmed by decades of cognitive research, the principle states that people best remember:

What they hear first (primacy)

What they hear last (recency)

And they're most likely to forget what happens in between.
In demo terms, that means your buyer is most likely to retain:

Your opening message—especially if it sets a clear expectation or solves an urgent problem.

Your closing recap or highlight—especially if it's framed as the big takeaway

But unless you've designed for it, much of the middle content may get lost in the noise. This has huge implications for how you structure your presentation. It means your most important ideas—the differentiators, emotional hooks, or strategic wins—should be placed early or late, never buried in the middle.

Unfortunately, many software demos follow a product-driven sequence. They walk through tabs, screens, or settings in the order the product was built—not in a way that aligns with the brain's natural memory curve. In this chapter, we'll fix that.

You'll learn how to restructure your demo to capitalize on primacy and recency—so the right ideas stick, the emotional moments land, and your message survives long after the call ends.

Section 2: Why Middle Segments Often Get Lost

The cognitive dead zone in most demos—and how to avoid it.

While the beginning and end of a demo enjoy the brain's attention spotlight, the middle often sinks into the shadows. This isn't about poor content—it's about how human cognition naturally works. Without deliberate reinforcement or emotional stimulation, the middle of any presentation is the easiest part to forget.

Why does this happen? It comes down to attention span and cognitive drift.

1. Mental Fatigue Sets In

By minute 10 or 15 of a demo, your buyer's working memory is taxed. They've already been absorbing new concepts, interpreting visuals, and juggling internal questions. If the middle of your demo lacks structure, relevance, or variation, their brain starts to disengage—not because they don't care, but because mental energy is finite.

2. Mid-Demo Multitasking

This is also when distractions kick in. Notifications pop up. A Slack message pings. They glance at their calendar. Without a compelling reason to stay mentally present, the buyer's focus fades—and they miss key information delivered midstream.

3. Overload and Feature Stacking

Many presenters load the middle with dense feature walkthroughs. They assume the buyer is "warmed up" and ready for technical depth. But in reality, this is where cognitive overload peaks. Rapid sequences of disconnected features make the brain abandon context and stop building memory altogether.

The takeaway: Don't bury your best content in the middle. Avoid long stretches without interaction, story, or recap. Instead, design the middle as a bridge—reinforcing the promise you made early and building anticipation for what's coming next.

In the next section, we'll look at how to open your demo with clarity, value, and impact—so you win the brain's attention early.

Section 3: Front-Loading Your Message with Meaning

Hook early, or risk losing the brain for the rest of the call.

The first few minutes of your demo are the most valuable real estate in the entire presentation. Why? Because primacy isn't just about being first—it's about framing everything that follows.

When you open with meaning—when you immediately show relevance, clarity, and value—the brain leans in. It decides: This matters. Pay attention.
But when you start with navigation, configurations, or introductions to your admin panel, the brain makes a different judgment: This looks complicated. Tune out.

What Belongs in the First Five Minutes?

1.   The Problem You Solve

"Most teams are drowning in intake emails. This is how we stop that—fast."

2.   The High-Value Outcome

"I'll show you how clients like yours cut admin time in half and got real-time reporting."

3.   The Quick Win

Give them an early visual payoff. One dashboard. One-click automation. Something that makes the viewer say, "Oh—that's nice."

Use an "Early Payoff" Hook

Don't wait to build suspense—deliver something useful up front. This could be a before/after transformation, a high-level report view, or a single screen that instantly simplifies the process.

Think of it like the movie trailer moment. You're not giving everything away—but you're showing just enough to keep them interested and wanting more.

If you can nail the first five minutes, everything after becomes easier to absorb. You've won attention—and the right to go deeper.

In the next section, we'll flip to the other end of the timeline: how to end with clarity, emotion, and a lasting impression.

Section 4: The Last 5 Minutes – How to Stick the Landing

End with clarity, not a cliffhanger.

The final moments of your demo are not just about wrapping up—they're about cementing what gets remembered. This is where the recency effect kicks in: the brain gives special weight to the last thing it hears.
Yet too many demos end with vague phrases like,
"So... any questions?"
or
"That's the system. Let us know what you think."
That's not a close. It's a fadeout.

Instead, your closing should restate the value, re-engage the emotion, and create momentum for what comes next. It should feel like a final chord in a song—not a PowerPoint slide that ran out of content.

What Belongs in the Last 5 Minutes?

1.   A Recap of Key Outcomes

"So to recap, we automated intake, centralized routing, and gave you real-time visibility across the team—all in under 30 minutes."

2.   A Clear Benefit Framing
"That means fewer bottlenecks, less manual tracking, and faster decision-making for your ops team."

3.   A Simple Visual or Phrase to Remember

"This is your morning command center. Everything your team needs, in one view."

4. A Confident Call to Action

"We'd love to set up a trial environment for your team to test. Who would be best to loop in?"

When the demo ends with clarity and conviction, the message travels better. Buyers can repeat it. Champions can advocate for it. And stakeholders can see its shape without being in the room.

In the next section, we'll look at how to structure the entire demo around memory—not menus—by anchoring it in story, not just software.

Section 5: Structuring for Memory, Not Features

Design your demo around how people think—not how products are built.

Most demos follow the product's architecture: you start with the dashboard, move to settings, then explore modules one by one. It's logical—from an engineering perspective. But it's not how the brain prefers to learn or remember.

Why? Because feature-based demos tend to feel disconnected. Buyers get a series of tools without a storyline. And without structure, memory fades fast.

Instead, the most effective demos are designed around use cases, outcomes, and transformation. They answer:

- "What problem does this solve?"
- "What changes for my team?"
- "Why should I care right now?"

Story First. Feature Second. Structure your demo like a narrative, not a product tour. Try this framework:

1. Set the stage – What challenge is the buyer facing?
2. Introduce the tool – Show the workflow that solves it.
3. Reveal the result – Highlight the win: saved time, fewer steps, better visibility.

Example:

"Let's say your team gets a customer complaint on Friday afternoon. Normally, that sits in email over the weekend. Here's how we capture it, route it, and have it resolved before Monday."

That structure is inherently memorable—because it mirrors how the brain understands events.

Anchor to Outcomes, Not Navigation:

Rather than saying:

"Now we'll look at the notification settings..."

Say:

"This is how your team gets instant alerts—so issues never fall through the cracks."

One is a tour. The other is a takeaway.

In the next section, we'll explore the power of bookending your message—why what you repeat at the beginning and end sticks better than anything in between.

Section 6: The Power of Bookending

Repeat it at the end—and the brain remembers it.

One of the simplest, most powerful techniques for enhancing demo recall is bookending—the act of repeating your core message at both the beginning and end of your presentation. Why does it work? Because repetition at emotionally and cognitively charged moments (the start and finish) gives your message double exposure during peak memory windows.

Bookending helps your buyer:

- Recognize the theme of the demo
- Tie features back to a larger outcome
- Retain and retell the key value proposition

Bookending in Practice:

At the beginning:

"Today, I'll show you how we eliminate the three biggest blockers in your intake process: speed, visibility, and accountability."

Then deliver your demo.

At the end:

"So just as we said up front—we streamlined speed, gave you visibility, and made every step accountable."

This mirrored framing closes the loop in the buyer's brain. It creates narrative cohesion. It transforms disconnected content into a story with a clear beginning, middle, and resolution.

Why It Works:
Bookending is effective because it supports semantic encoding—the process by which information becomes meaningful and memorable. When the brain encounters a message twice, especially wrapped in emotion or significance, it flags it as important.
In short: Repetition = Reinforcement. And strategic placement = Stickiness. Don't just hope your buyer remembers your core message. Engineer it.

In the next section, we'll explore how pacing and rhythm—not speed—help reduce overload and support memory retention throughout your demo.

Section 7: Pacing for Cognitive Rhythm

Why slower, more deliberate delivery improves retention.

Most demos move too fast—not because the presenter is in a rush, but because they're deeply familiar with the content. What feels like a reasonable pace to you can feel like an avalanche to your buyer, especially if they're seeing the product for the first time.

Cognitive science tells us the brain doesn't just need information—it needs time to process, connect, and store it. That's where pacing becomes a performance lever. The right rhythm helps your buyer stay engaged, absorb meaning, and remember what matters.

What Is Cognitive Rhythm?

It's the mental tempo at which people process information. If you deliver too much, too quickly, without pauses or transitions, the brain can't keep up. The result? Overload. Fog. Forgetting.
But when you introduce ideas one at a time, with short pauses to reinforce and reflect, you create a rhythm the brain can follow—and a message it can retain.

Tactics for Better Pacing in Your Demo

- Pause after key actions
"Let me stop here for a second. Notice how that alert was automatically created."

- Slow down at transitions
"Before we move into reporting, let's recap what we've seen so far..."

- Let moments breathe
Don't rush a big reveal. Let silence do some of the work.

- Watch for nonverbal signals
If your buyer leans back, looks confused, or stops nodding—slow down.

Good pacing isn't slow. It's intentional. It makes your demo feel confident, clear, and thoughtfully delivered.
Next, we'll explore how to strategically insert questions and pauses to break the flow, reset attention, and reinforce memory.

Section 8: Strategic Use of Pauses and Questions

Interrupt the flow to strengthen memory and increase engagement.

While most demos are structured around what to show and what to say, few presenters think about when to pause. Yet well-timed pauses and intentional questions are powerful cognitive tools. They give the brain a moment to catch up, process, and retain.

In a fast-paced, screen-share-heavy environment, the buyer is often scrambling to keep up. Strategic pauses aren't dead air—they're opportunities for reflection, learning, and emotional reset.

Why Pauses Work:
Pauses provide processing time. They reduce mental load and prevent the brain from dumping earlier content. They also give weight to what was just said—turning a moment into a memory. Examples:

- After a demo of a simplified workflow:
"Let's pause here. What's standing out to you so far?"

- After showing a before-and-after impact:
"That's a big shift—take a second to think about how your team might respond."

These pauses don't slow things down—they deepen them.

Questions That Reset and Re-engage:

Asking the right questions mid-demo does three things:

89

1. Checks for understanding
"Does this flow match how your team works now?"

2. Invites relevance
"Would this replace any of your current steps?"

3. Reactivates attention
"Want to see how that logic ties into reporting?"

These questions prompt internal thinking—even if the buyer doesn't answer aloud. That internal engagement boosts retention and makes the demo feel conversational, not scripted.

Next, we'll explore how to bring all of this together into a simple, repeatable structure—the 3-part Cognitive Demo Flow.

Section 9: Building the 3-Part Cognitive Demo Flow

A simple structure that matches how the brain prefers to learn.

If you want your demos to be not just seen but remembered, they need structure—not based on feature sets, but based on how people learn. One of the most effective models for this is the 3-Part Cognitive Demo Flow. It's built around how the brain retains information, transitions attention, and stores meaning.
Think of it as a rhythm: Engage → Explain → Elevate.

Part 1: Engage (Set Expectations + Quick Win)

This is your chance to:
- Frame the problem
- Preview the solution

- Deliver an early, visual payoff

Example:

"Let me show you the exact screen that helped a similar client reduce intake volume by 40%."

The goal is to earn attention quickly and establish relevance within the first 5 minutes.

Part 2: Explain (Problem–Solution Walkthrough)

Now you guide the audience through a clear, paced experience:
- Focus on 2–3 core workflows
- Tie each step to a real-world outcome
- Use narrative and visuals to simplify complexity

This is the heart of your demo—but it's also where you must manage cognitive load carefully.

Part 3: Elevate (Recap + Outcome Framing)
The final section is about reinforcement:
- Recap what was covered
- Emphasize emotional and business value
- Preview next steps confidently

Example:

"So we automated intake, created visibility, and gave your execs real-time control—all without adding friction."

This flow respects how the brain processes time, tension, and memory. It turns demos into stories with structure—not product tours with click paths.

Let's finish this chapter with a mindset shift: how to think like a memory architect in every demo you deliver.

Section 10: Demo Like a Memory Architect

Design every moment for impact, retention, and repeatability.

The best demo presenters aren't just storytellers or product experts—they're memory architects. They understand that what gets remembered is what gets repeated. And what gets repeated is what gets acted on.

If your demo only delivers information, you leave retention to chance. But if you build your presentation with the brain in mind, you control what sticks—and give your buyer the tools to carry your message forward.

What It Means to Think Like a Memory Architect:

It means structuring your demo intentionally:

- You place key ideas at the beginning and end—where the brain remembers best.
- You use storytelling, visuals, and repetition to encode meaning.
- You pace your delivery with pauses and reflection, not just speed.

And you don't just show features—you design moments. Moments that solve problems. Moments that create relief. Moments that make buyers say,

"I can't wait to show this to my team."

Primacy–Recency Checklist:

Before your next demo, ask:
- What's my opening hook? (Primacy)
- What emotional moment can I deliver early?
- What's my closing message? (Recency)
- What do I want them to remember—and repeat?

If you don't plan these moments, they won't happen by accident.

The good news? Most sellers aren't thinking this way. That means every memory-aligned demo you deliver becomes a competitive advantage.

In the next chapter, we'll break things down further, showing how to split your content into cognitive chunks that reduce overwhelm and improve clarity at every stage.

Chapter 6: Chunking

Teach faster, sell clearer, and reduce overload through cognitive segmentation.

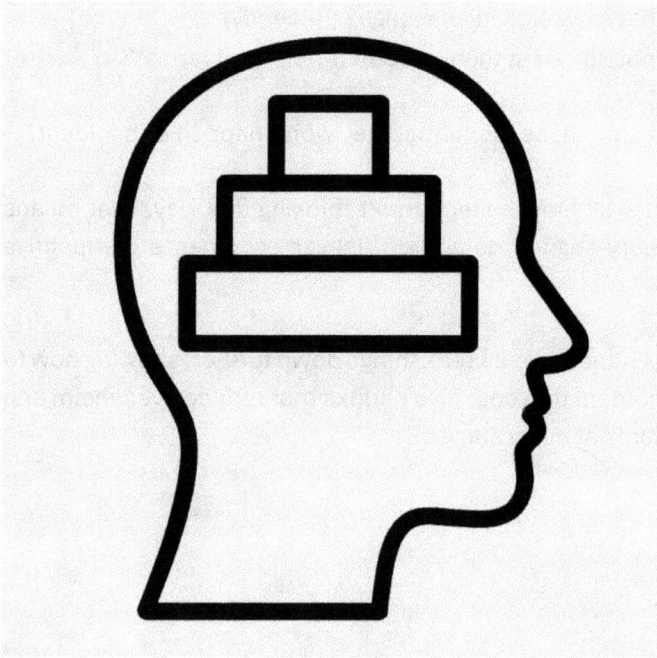

Section 1: What Is Chunking—and Why It Works

How grouping content makes demos easier to follow, remember, and repeat.

"Chunking" is a term borrowed from cognitive psychology that refers to grouping information into small, meaningful units. It's how the brain naturally learns. Rather than processing a flood of scattered details, the brain prefers to absorb information in organized segments, each with a clear identity and purpose. Think of how we remember a phone number. Instead of trying to memorize 10 digits in a row—3478120956—we break it into chunks: (347)–812–0956. Same data, radically easier to retain.

Why Chunking Works in Software Demos:

Chunking reduces cognitive load by helping your audience:
- Focus on one concept at a time
- Connect related information more easily
- Store and recall ideas more effectively

This is especially critical in demos, where buyers are simultaneously learning, evaluating, and comparing. If you present five workflows back-to-back without structure, the brain tries to keep up—and fails. But if you deliver three chunks, each with a theme and a natural entry and exit, the brain locks them in more easily.

In Practice: What Is a Demo Chunk?

A "chunk" in a demo might be:
- A specific workflow (e.g., "Submit to Approve")
- A user role's experience (e.g., "What your manager sees")

- A business problem and how your product solves it

The key is framing—introducing each chunk clearly, delivering it with focus, and transitioning cleanly to the next.

In the sections ahead, we'll explore how most demos fail to chunk, and how to apply chunking techniques based on workflows, personas, and real-world problems.

Section 2: The Cost of Unchunked Demos

Why your audience forgets what you said five minutes ago.

Most demos feel longer than they are—not because of duration, but because of mental strain. When you walk your buyer through a nonstop stream of screens, features, and options without clear breaks, you create a cognitive mess. The brain doesn't know where one idea ends and another begins. It can't store it, and it certainly can't retell it later.

This is what happens in unchunked demos—and it's more common than most presenters realize.

What Unchunked Looks Like:
- Jumping from feature to feature without transitions
- Covering five tools in 10 minutes with no organizing principle
- Using navigation order (e.g., top menu left to right) instead of purpose-driven structure

From your perspective, you're "showing everything." From theirs, you're "dumping information."

The result? Buyers disengage, forget, and fail to act.

Why It Fails:

1. Working memory gets overwhelmed
    The human brain can hold only a few items at once—
    especially under pressure or distraction.
2. No natural stopping points
    Without mental breaks, the audience never gets to reset or
    reflect.
3. No anchors for recall
    Unchunked content lacks mental "folders," so the buyer
    can't retrieve what they heard—even if they were engaged
    at the time.

Here's the scary truth: even strong demos can be forgotten if
they're delivered without structure. The good news? With
chunking, you not only reduce overload—you make your message
easier to remember, easier to share, and easier to champion
internally.

Up next: how to structure your demo around workflows—the most
intuitive way to chunk your message.

Section 3: Chunking by Workflow

The most intuitive way to organize your demo—and align with real-world use.

One of the simplest and most effective chunking strategies is to
organize your demo around workflows. Why? Because workflows
mirror how your buyer thinks. They represent action, purpose, and
outcome—the way real people use your software to get real work
done.
Buyers don't think in terms of tabs or modules. They think in terms
of, "How do I do this job faster, better, or with fewer errors?"

That's why demonstrating complete workflows—start to finish—creates clarity. It gives the buyer context, continuity, and a reason to care.

What Makes a Workflow Chunk?

A workflow chunk includes:
- A clear starting point (e.g., a submitted request)
- A series of actions or decisions
- A clear result or outcome (e.g., approval, alert, report)

Example chunk:
"Let's walk through how a new intake request is captured, routed, and tracked until resolution."
This structure gives the brain a storyline: beginning, middle, end.
It's far easier to retain than a scattered tour of settings or features.

Why This Works So Well
1. It aligns with job tasks buyers already perform
2. It helps reduce switching cost—mentally and visually
3. It bundles multiple features into one meaningful unit

Even complex systems feel simpler when framed through the lens of purposeful work.
To apply this in your next demo:

- Identify 2–3 key workflows most relevant to the buyer
- Walk through each as its own "chapter"
- Label them clearly as you transition in and out

Up next, we'll show how to chunk your content by persona or role—so each stakeholder hears what matters most to them.

Section 4: Chunking by Role or Persona

Tailoring the demo to each stakeholder's world.

In a typical demo, you're not presenting to one brain—you're presenting to several. A frontline user, a department manager, and an executive each bring different concerns, levels of detail, and emotional triggers. One of the best ways to keep everyone engaged and reduce confusion is to chunk your demo by persona.

This approach means delivering discrete, labeled sections tailored to each stakeholder's role—so they know when to tune in and what applies to them.

Why Chunking by Role Works:

1. It increases relevance. Each buyer hears content meant specifically for them.
2. It prevents overwhelm. Stakeholders don't have to filter what's "for them" in real time.
3. It improves advocacy. When they feel understood, they're more likely to champion your solution.

Instead of blending everything into one generic walkthrough, you signal intent:
"Now let's switch to the operations manager view. This is where most team leaders spend their time."
That statement sets an expectation, creates focus, and validates that stakeholder's role.

How to Structure Persona-Based Chunks:

- For users: Show ease of use, speed, and automation

- For managers: Highlight visibility, task tracking, and bottleneck reduction
- For execs: Emphasize outcomes, reporting, and strategic alignment
- For IT/admins: Focus on control, security, and integration

Each chunk should last 3–5 minutes and be framed with an opening and closing phrase to clearly segment it.

If your audience is mixed, let each role know when "their moment" is coming—and when they can take a mental breather. Next, we'll explore how to chunk your demo by problem-solution patterns—a powerful structure for persuasion.

Section 5: Chunking by Problem–Solution Pattern

Structure your demo like a diagnosis—with a cure.

Another high-impact way to chunk your demo is by using a problem–solution format. Instead of walking through tools in isolation, you frame each segment around a specific challenge your buyer faces—and then show exactly how your software solves it.

This method taps into the brain's love of story. Every good story starts with tension (the problem), escalates with action (your demo), and resolves with outcome (the solution). When your buyer sees the pain and the relief packaged together, they don't just understand it—they feel it.

Why This Works:
1. It validates the buyer's world. You're showing you understand their pain.

2. It keeps attention. The brain wants to know how the story ends.
3. It elevates relevance. You're not just showing features—you're solving something that matters.

Example:

"One common pain point we hear is that approvals get stuck in inboxes. Let me show you how our dynamic routing eliminates that delay."

That's a full chunk: problem, solution, and emotional payoff—all in under five minutes.

How to Build These Chunks:

- Identify your top 3–5 buyer pain points
- Pair each one with a feature or workflow that addresses it
- Label each segment clearly, e.g.,

"Now let's look at how we solve manual intake tracking."

- End each chunk with a result statement:

"This reduces average resolution time by 42%."

These chunks are story-ready. They're easier for your buyer to remember—and easier to repeat inside their organization.

Up next, we'll explore how to connect your chunks with clear transitions and signposts that guide the brain and reduce mental friction.

Section 6: Signposting Between Chunks

Guide the brain with clear transitions—just like chapters in a book.

Even the best chunked content can lose impact if the transitions between segments are clumsy or invisible. The brain needs signals to reset, reorient, and prepare for what's next. That's why great demos use signposting—short, intentional phrases that mark the start and end of each demo segment.

Think of signposting as your cognitive GPS. It tells your buyer where they are, what's coming, and how it connects to the big picture. Without it, even well-structured demos can feel like a blur.

Examples of Signposting in Action:
Before a new chunk:
"Now that we've seen how requests are submitted, let's take a look at how they're routed to the right team member."

At the end of a chunk:

"So that's how we eliminate intake chaos with automated triage."

When changing persona focus:

"Next, let's shift into the manager view so you can see how leaders track team performance."

These are short, low-effort statements—but they make a massive difference in audience clarity and retention.

Why the Brain Loves Signposts:

1. They provide structure. Buyers know what to expect.
2. They reduce load. The brain doesn't have to guess what's happening.
3. They aid memory. Chunks are easier to recall when labeled.

Pro tip: use consistent language when labeling segments, like "Let's walk through the approval process" or "This next piece is for your finance team."

Transitions don't need to be flashy. They just need to be intentional.

In the next section, we'll reinforce memory inside each chunk with targeted repetition and recap strategies.

Section 7: Repetition Within and Between Chunks

Say it again—strategically.

One of the biggest mistakes in demos is assuming once is enough. You explain a feature. You show a workflow. You name a benefit. And then... you move on. But the brain doesn't learn that way. It needs repetition—not random, but deliberate and well-placed. Within a chunk, repetition reinforces clarity. Between chunks, it creates cohesion. Across the entire demo, it turns complexity into memory.

Why Strategic Repetition Matters:

- Repetition signals importance to the brain.
- It increases recall and improves the buyer's ability to retell what they saw.
- It allows the buyer to connect the dots—across screens, use cases, and outcomes.

Example within a chunk:
"You'll notice this same auto-triage logic applies to every intake type, not just customer service."
Example between chunks:
"Just like we saw in approvals, reporting also pulls from those same routing rules—so your data is always in sync."

Types of Useful Demo Repetition:
1. Terminology repetition
    Use consistent names for features or roles to reduce
    ambiguity.
"Let's go back to the Smart Queue again..."

2. Outcome repetition
    Restate the value multiple times, in slightly different
    words.
"Faster approvals. Fewer emails. More transparency."

3. Visual repetition
    Refer back to screens you've already shown to connect
    concepts.
"Remember that dashboard we saw earlier? Here's how it gets
populated."

Think of repetition as a memory multiplier. Done right, it makes
your message stickier without sounding redundant.

Up next: how to manage pacing inside each chunk so your
message comes through clearly—without rushing or losing focus.

Section 8: Pacing Each Chunk for Maximum Clarity

Slowing down doesn't mean dumbing down.

Even with well-structured chunks, your demo can fall flat if each
one is rushed. The brain needs time to absorb a new idea,
especially when it's complex or layered. That's why pacing—within
each chunk—is critical.
Think of pacing like paragraph spacing in a book. Without enough
room between ideas, everything blurs. But when you pause, recap,

and move deliberately, the content becomes digestible, clear, and memorable.

How to Pace a Demo Chunk:

1.   Start with an entry phrase
"Let's walk through the full workflow for submitting a request."

2.   Deliver one idea at a time
     Avoid stacking features or jumping ahead. Keep each point clean and focused.

3.   Pause for observation or comment
"Notice how the user is guided automatically—no manual routing needed."

4.   Summarize before moving on
"So that chunk covers submission through auto-assignment. Let's now look at escalation handling."
Each step gives your buyer room to follow the logic and build understanding.

Why This Works:
- It reduces cognitive saturation. Too much, too fast = mental drop-off.
- It keeps the buyer emotionally engaged. They feel guided, not overwhelmed.
- It gives room for questions—or for silent processing.

Pro tip: If you're not sure how fast to go, match your pace to the buyer's body language or verbal response time. If they're quiet, nodding, or asking clarifying questions, you're probably on track. If they're silent and frozen, you're likely speeding ahead.

The takeaway? One idea per chunk. Delivered at the buyer's pace.

Up next, we'll explore how to adapt chunking for demos of different lengths—so you stay effective whether you have 15, 30, or 60 minutes.

Section 9: Adapting Chunks for Different Demo Lengths

How to stay structured whether you have 60 minutes—or 6.

One of the greatest strengths of chunking is its flexibility. Whether you're delivering a 60-minute deep dive or a 15-minute discovery call, chunks allow you to adjust scope without sacrificing clarity. Instead of trimming randomly or rushing through everything, you simply choose which chunks to include—and which to save for later. This makes your demo more agile, more tailored, and far less overwhelming.

For 60-Minute Demos:
- Include 3–5 major chunks
- Go deeper into each, with workflows, persona views, and problem framing
- Allow time for interaction after each chunk
- End with a full recap and next steps

Example Structure:
1. Workflow: Intake to Approval
2. Persona: Manager View
3. Problem: Reducing Resolution Time
4. Workflow: Reporting & Dashboards
5. Outcome Recap + CTA

For 30-Minute Demos:

- Select your top 2–3 chunks based on buyer priority
- Skip redundant personas or edge-case features
- Keep transitions tight and end with a strong summary

Example:

1. Problem: Missed Tickets
2. Workflow: Triage to Assignment
3. Outcome: SLA Visibility

For 15-Minute Executive Overviews
- Use a single, high-impact chunk with big-picture framing
- Lead with outcomes, not features
- Preview other chunks without going deep

Example:

"Today I'll show you just one thing—how we reduced response times by 40% through automation. Everything else builds from that foundation."

The chunking method gives you modular control over your content—so your message stays sharp, no matter how much time you have.

Next, we'll close the chapter by showing how to think of your demo not as a linear tour—but as a modular story you can tailor in real time.

Section 10: The Chunked Demo as a Modular Story

Think less like a presenter—more like a navigator.

The best demos aren't rigid walkthroughs. They're modular stories—flexible, dynamic, and guided by what the buyer needs in the moment. That's the true power of chunking: it frees you from the script and gives you a toolkit of purposeful segments you can mix, match, and reorder as needed.

You're not locked into a single path. You're navigating a set of problem-solving episodes, each with its own internal logic, value, and memory hook.

How to Think Modularly:

Your chunks are chapters, not steps. This mindset shift helps you:
- Adapt live to questions or stakeholder shifts
- Cut or expand chunks based on time
- Stay focused without getting lost in feature creep

Example:

The CFO joins 10 minutes in? Skip the workflow and jump to the "Finance Dashboard" chunk.

The buyer says they're only evaluating intake solutions? Focus on the "Routing & Prioritization" chunk.

Your New Role: Demo Navigator:

As a memory architect, your role isn't to show everything—it's to guide your buyer through the right chunks, at the right pace, in the right sequence for them.

This elevates your presence from product expert to consultative guide—someone who doesn't just know the tool, but understands how people learn, decide, and remember.

In the next chapter, we'll explore how to design demo moments that trigger emotion—because logic makes people think, but emotion makes them act.

Chapter 7: Cognitive Accelerator

How to move buyers from interest to action by triggering the right feelings.

Section 1: Why Emotion Drives Decision-Making

Because logic doesn't lead—emotion does.

We like to think of B2B decisions as rational, objective, and data-driven. But neuroscience tells a different story. The truth is: emotion leads, logic follows. Even in complex enterprise deals, emotion is the spark that ignites memory, frames judgment, and triggers momentum. The brain's decision-making engine—centered in the limbic system—is wired to prioritize emotionally salient input. That means what *feels* important gets processed, retained, and acted upon. What doesn't? It fades.

The Neuroscience Behind Emotional Memory:
Studies show that emotionally charged experiences are more likely to be:

- Noticed
- Encoded into long-term memory
- Shared with others

Why? Because the brain tags those moments as meaningful. When something relieves stress, creates delight, or inspires trust, it activates the amygdala and enhances hippocampal activity—boosting memory retention and shaping decisions. In contrast, neutral, data-heavy demos—no matter how accurate—often fail to make a lasting impression.

The Implication for Demos:

If your demo is flat—even if it's flawless—it risks being forgettable. But when you create moments that move people, you become memorable.

For example:

- Showing a clunky "before" screen, then revealing a sleek, automated view triggers relief and surprise.
- Naming a pain point they haven't articulated creates a sense of recognition and trust.
- Telling a 30-second story about a real user's success taps into hope and confidence.

These emotional signals tell the brain: *This matters. Remember this. Act on this.* Emotion doesn't replace logic in a demo—it clears the path for it. In the next section, we'll unpack the specific emotions that drive B2B decisions and how to use them intentionally.

Section 2: The Most Powerful Emotions in B2B Demos

What your buyer really wants to feel—and what to avoid at all costs.

Emotion drives action—but not all emotions are equal in the context of a software demo. Some spark energy, clarity, and trust. Others trigger confusion, resistance, or disengagement. Your job as a presenter is to amplify the right emotional responses—and eliminate the wrong ones.

Let's look at the four emotions that create movement in the buyer's mind—and the three that kill deals.

Emotions That Accelerate Buying:

1. Relief – "Finally, a way to stop the madness."
   Relief is powerful. It tells the brain: the pain can end. It shows that your product solves a real, lingering issue.

2. Excitement – "This changes the game."
   A feature surprise, a clean dashboard, or an automation that eliminates busywork can light up the buyer's imagination.

3. Confidence – "This will work for us."
   Confidence comes from clarity, clean workflows, and seeing their exact needs reflected in your solution.

4. Trust – "These people get us."
   Built through empathy, personalization, and human delivery. It's not what you show—it's how you show it.

Emotions That Sabotage Memory and Momentum:

1. Confusion – Too much, too fast, too technical.

2. Boredom – Long explanations, lifeless tone, no payoff.

3. Anxiety – Unclear next steps, complexity, or uncertainty.

These negative emotions don't just dull the experience—they actively interfere with retention and recall. Buyers forget what confused or stressed them. They also hesitate to re-engage.

In the next section, we'll show how to map emotions to demo moments—so every phase of your presentation intentionally supports the buyer's emotional journey.

Section 3: Mapping Emotions to Demo Moments

Design each moment to trigger a feeling—not just a thought.

High-impact demos aren't emotional accidents. They're emotional journeys. Just like a great movie or speech, the best demos are mapped to emotional beats—carefully planned moments designed to evoke relief, surprise, clarity, or confidence at just the right time. Instead of asking, "What should I show here?" try asking, "What should they feel here?" That mindset shift is what separates product tours from persuasive experiences.

The Emotional Flow of a Winning Demo

1. The Hook (Relief)
    - Moment: You name their pain—clearly and confidently.
    - Emotion: "Yes. That's exactly what we're dealing with."
    - Outcome: They lean in. You're speaking their language.
2. The First Feature (Surprise)

- o   Moment: You reveal something fast, visual, and delightful.
- o   Emotion: "Whoa, that's slick."
- o   Outcome: Curiosity spikes. You've bought their attention.

3. The Deep Dive (Confidence)
- o   Moment: You walk through the solution calmly, clearly.
- o   Emotion: "This is doable. This fits us."
- o   Outcome: Resistance drops. Vision builds.

4. The Personal Insight (Trust)
- o   Moment: You reflect something unique about their workflow or team.
- o   Emotion: "They really listened."
- o   Outcome: The human connection deepens.

5. The Outcome Frame (Hope)
- o   Moment: You show what life looks like post-implementation.
- o   Emotion: "We could actually get there."
- o   Outcome: Emotional momentum.

By assigning an emotional target to each phase of your demo, you create not just understanding, but buy-in.

Next, we'll dive into how to use storytelling as your emotional engine—because stories do what slides can't.

Section 4: Storytelling as an Emotional Engine

Because people forget features—but they remember stories.

If you want your demo to move people, don't just explain—tell a story. Stories are the brain's native language. They bypass analytical defenses and go straight to the emotional core, where attention, empathy, and memory live.

In sales demos, storytelling isn't about spinning fiction—it's about wrapping facts in emotionally resonant context. It helps the buyer see themselves in the scenario, feel the pain, and imagine the resolution.

Why Stories Work:

- They create emotional immersion—the buyer steps into the scene.
- They improve recall—narrative structure sticks better than lists.
- They build trust—you're showing understanding, not just expertise.

A story activates both cognitive and emotional regions of the brain. It creates a dual encoding effect, increasing the chance that your buyer will remember—and retell—what they heard.

Simple Story Formats for Demos

1. Before and After

"This team used to spend 8 hours a week chasing tickets. Now? They don't touch them—everything's auto-routed."

2. Day in the Life

"Here's what a frontline rep sees when they log in on Monday morning..."

3. Success Snapshot

"A client just like you went live last quarter. Within two weeks, they cut intake time by 30%."

Keep it short. Keep it specific. One powerful story does more than five perfectly delivered slides.

When you wrap your demo in stories, you shift from demoing software to showing transformation.

Next, we'll cover how your tone, voice, and timing influence emotion—sometimes even more than your content.

Section 5: Using Voice, Tone, and Timing to Influence Feeling

It's not just what you say—it's how you say it.

Emotion is contagious. The way you speak—your tone, rhythm, and energy—transmits feeling faster than any slide. In fact, your delivery often shapes the buyer's emotional response more than your content does.

A rushed voice signals pressure. A calm tone signals control. A deliberate pause can create anticipation or give weight to a statement. When your voice aligns with your message, the emotional impact multiplies.

Tone Tips for Emotional Impact:

- Warmth builds trust

  Speak like you're helping a colleague—not reading a pitch. "Let me show you something that really helped one of our clients…"

- Confidence creates clarity

  Avoid filler words or hesitant phrasing. Own your message. "You'll see how this replaces three manual steps—with no extra training needed."

- Curiosity sparks curiosity

  Use tonal variation to create energy around key moments. "Here's where it gets interesting…"

The Power of Pauses:

Silence isn't awkward—it's powerful. A pause:

- Highlights the point you just made
- Gives your buyer time to process
- Signals that this moment matters

Example:

"This dashboard used to take four hours to compile manually. [Pause] Now? It updates in real time."

Let that moment land.

The goal isn't to become a performer—it's to become intentional. Every tone choice either amplifies or mutes the emotional signal you're trying to send.

In the next section, we'll design emotional "aha" moments—the turning points that stick in memory long after your demo ends.

Section 6: Designing Emotional "Aha" Moments

Make your demo unforgettable—with one well-placed moment of magic.

Not every moment in a demo needs to sparkle—but one should. The best demos contain at least one emotional peak: a moment of insight, relief, or excitement so clear and visceral that the buyer remembers it without effort.

These "aha" moments aren't accidents. They're engineered— through setup, contrast, timing, and delivery.

What Makes an 'Aha' Moment?

1.   A clear before-and-after contrast

"This is what your team deals with today... Now here's what happens when our automation kicks in."

2.   A feature that solves a high-friction pain

"Remember the bottleneck we talked about? This kills it— completely."

3.   A surprising simplification

"All of that happens with one click. No scripts. No IT."

4.   A visual reveal

"Let me show you what your execs will see—real-time metrics, no spreadsheets."

These moments land because they trigger a strong emotional response: relief, hope, amazement, or confidence.

Why They Work:

- The brain remembers peaks more than averages
- Emotionally charged moments get encoded faster
- Buyers retell the moment internally—spreading your message

Your job is to set up the tension, deliver the payoff clearly, then pause. Let it breathe.

Example:

"This view right here? That's what saved our last client 20 hours a week. Every week."

Let silence follow. Let their mind absorb it.

You don't need ten "wow" moments. You need one that sticks.

Up next, we'll look at the opposite challenge—how to avoid emotional flatlines that leave your demo forgettable.

Section 7: Avoiding Emotional Flatlines

How even great demos can fall flat—and what to do instead.

The silent killer of sales demos isn't error. It's emotional neutrality. If your demo is technically perfect but emotionally flat, it won't be remembered, championed, or acted upon. It will fade into the background noise of the buyer's week—just another meeting, another tool.

Emotional flatlines happen when every moment feels the same. Same tone, same pace, same screen, same voice. No spikes. No shifts. No story. Just steady, polite forgettability.

How to Spot a Flat Demo:

- No visible or verbal reaction from the audience
- No questions or comments until the very end
- No standout moments for the buyer to latch onto
- The presenter sounds identical from start to finish
- The product is explained—but never felt

Flat demos are often over-scripted, overly safe, or focused entirely on features, not meaning.

How to Fix It:

1. Add narrative contrast
   Don't just show "how it works"—show "how it changes lives." Use stories and problem framing.
2. Vary your delivery
   Mix calm explanation with excited emphasis. Use silence strategically.

3. Create at least one emotional spike

   Surprise. Relief. Recognition. Build to something worth remembering.

4. React to your audience

   If they lean in, pause. If they laugh, acknowledge it. Make it human.

The key is not constant excitement—it's emotional rhythm. Highs and lows. Energy and space. Peaks and pacing.

In the next section, we'll shift toward the most trust-building emotion in B2B sales: empathy—and how to harness it deliberately.

Section 8: Empathy as a Trust Lever

The fastest path to connection—and conversion.

If emotion drives action, then empathy drives trust. And trust is the foundation of any decision involving risk, money, or change—which describes nearly every B2B software deal. In a demo, empathy is what signals:

"We understand you. We've seen this before. We're not just selling—we're solving."

Empathy isn't softness. It's precision. It means tuning in, reflecting the buyer's world accurately, and adjusting your delivery based on what they're feeling—not just what they're saying.

Why Empathy Matters in Demos:

- It lowers defensiveness. Buyers stop bracing for the pitch.
- It increases engagement. People listen to those who understand them.
- It builds credibility. When you reflect their reality, you earn permission to guide change.

Ways to Demonstrate Empathy Live:

1. Name their pain before they do

"You're probably drowning in intake emails that never get tracked—right?"

2. Reflect their language

Use the same words and acronyms they use.

"Let's go back to that SLA you mentioned earlier."

3. Validate their reactions

"That's a fair concern. Other clients had the same hesitation before rollout."

4. Acknowledge the human cost

"What I'm showing you isn't just faster—it's about giving your team back their time."

Empathy isn't added—it's embedded. It's how you choose to speak, listen, and frame every chunk of your demo.

In the next section, we'll learn how to end your demo on an emotional high note—so your buyer leaves not just informed, but energized.

Section 9: Ending with Emotional Clarity
Leave them not just informed—but energized and ready to act.

The close of your demo is more than a recap. It's a psychological imprint—a final moment that shapes how the buyer remembers everything you showed. If you end flat or vague, the emotional energy you built evaporates. But if you end with clarity, confidence, and momentum, the buyer leaves feeling empowered.
You're not just summarizing. You're sealing the feeling.

What Emotional Clarity Sounds Like:
1.   "Here's what this means for you."
     Tie the demo back to their pain and goals.
"You're now seeing a system that can cut response times by half—with no extra headcount."
2.   "This is where teams usually see the biggest win."
     Anchor the emotion to a result.
"Most of our clients report the biggest relief in the first two weeks—once intake chaos disappears."
3.   "Let's talk next steps."
     A clear call to action gives direction and closure.

"If this feels aligned, let's set up a session with your operations lead."

Why the Ending Matters:

- The brain follows the Recency Effect—it remembers what came last.
- A confident close increases perceived credibility.
- Emotional resolution reduces indecision and builds forward motion.

End on a high note that reflects your message, matches their mindset, and leaves them thinking:

"This wasn't just a product—it was a solution we can actually feel."

In our final section, we'll tie everything together by creating a reusable emotional blueprint—a structure you can apply to every demo you deliver.

Section 10: The Emotional Blueprint of a High-Impact Demo

A repeatable pattern for connection, clarity, and conversion.

You've now explored how emotion fuels attention, memory, and action. But how do you operationalize that insight? How do you bring it into every demo, every time? The answer is a simple yet powerful framework: the Emotional Blueprint.

This isn't a script. It's a map—a sequence of emotional beats that shape how your buyer feels from start to finish.

The 5 Emotional Beats of a Cognitive Demo:
1. Recognition (Empathy + Relief)
    o Start by naming their world and their pain.
    o Emotion triggered: "They get it."
2. Surprise (Excitement + Possibility)
    o Show a moment of transformation—something they didn't expect.
    o Emotion triggered: "Wait, we can do that?"
3. Understanding (Confidence + Clarity)
    o Walk through your core value chunk-by-chunk with clean delivery.
    o Emotion triggered: "I can see how this works for us."
4. Connection (Trust + Personalization)
    o Reflect something unique about their goals, team, or workflow.
    o Emotion triggered: "They really listened."
5. Momentum (Hope + Direction)
    o Close with a clear, confident vision of what's next.
    o Emotion triggered: "Let's move forward."

How to Use This Framework:

Before every demo:

- Plan your emotional intent for each major chunk
- Design at least one "aha" moment
- Craft a closing that feels earned and optimistic

This blueprint ensures your demo doesn't just land logically—it resonates emotionally.

In the next chapter, we'll move from emotion to attention, diving into how to manage cognitive focus in a world full of distractions.

Chapter 8: Attention in a Distracted World

How to keep buyers focused when their brains—and inboxes—are working against you.

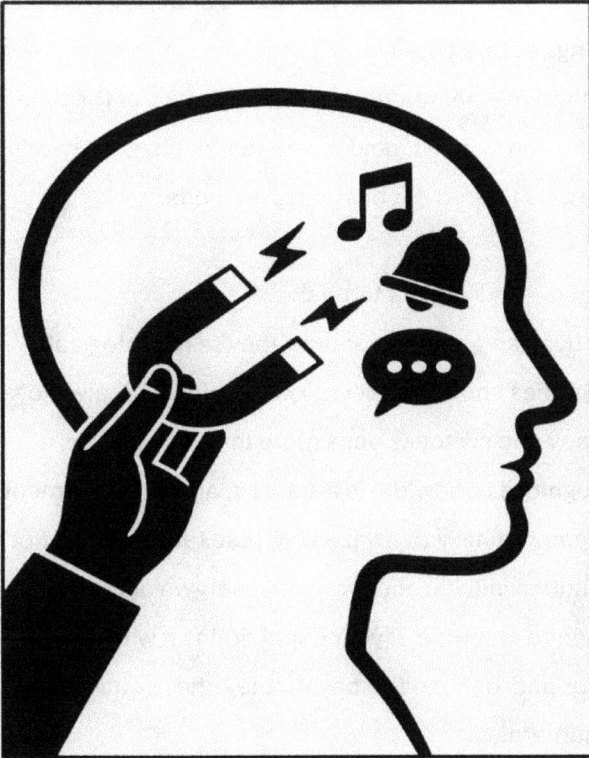

Section 1: Why Attention Is the New Currency

If you don't have attention, you don't have a demo.

We used to think the biggest challenge in sales was explaining the product clearly. But in today's environment, clarity is meaningless if your buyer isn't mentally present. And let's be honest—they're not. Most buyers walk into a demo with half a brain still on email, or the five meetings before yours.

That's why attention—not features—is the currency of the demo economy. If you can't earn it, hold it, and redirect it when needed, your message gets filtered out before it ever lands.

What's Changed—and Why It Matters:

The modern buyer isn't just distracted—they're neurologically overloaded. Studies show the average professional receives over 100 emails a day and switches apps more than 1,000 times a week. Their cognitive bandwidth is fractured, and every moment of your demo is competing with a dozen invisible tabs. And it's not just about multitasking. It's about mental energy. Your buyer's attention is a finite resource. If your demo drains it without delivering emotional or cognitive payoff, they check out—even if they stay on camera.

The Hidden Cost of Inattention:

- Missed value moments

- Poor recall in internal recap meetings
- Lower perceived product simplicity
- Weak emotional engagement
- Delayed or stalled decision-making

Most demos don't fail because the product isn't a fit—they fail because the buyer never truly engaged.

In this chapter, we'll explore how to design and deliver demos that respect the brain's attention span—and how to guide focus like a cognitive spotlight.

Up next: the Three Layers of Buyer Attention and how to design for each.

Section 2: The Three Layers of Buyer Attention

To manage attention, you must understand how deep it goes.

Not all attention is created equal. During a demo, your buyer isn't just "paying attention" or "not paying attention." Their focus exists on a spectrum—and your job is to guide them through it, moment by moment.

Think of attention as a three-layered system, like concentric rings. At each layer, your buyer becomes more engaged, more emotionally invested, and more likely to remember what you show.

Layer 1: Surface Attention:

This is the default state. The buyer hears your voice, sees the screen, but their mind is skimming. They're catching words, maybe multitasking. Surface attention is fragile and reactive—easy to gain, easy to lose.

Your goal here: capture. Use hooks, bold visuals, problem statements.

"Let me show you the biggest bottleneck we hear about from teams like yours."

Layer 2: Sustained Attention:
Now you've got them. Their eyes are tracking. Their mind is following your logic. You've earned a stretch of focused engagement. But it's still conditional—if the pace slows, the relevance drops, or the screen gets cluttered, they'll slip back.

Your goal here: maintain. Use chunking, framing, pacing.

"Here's the workflow, step-by-step—this part will really matter to your finance lead."

Layer 3: Deep Attention:
This is rare air. The buyer isn't just listening—they're processing, personalizing, and remembering. They're already thinking about how it applies to them. Emotion is activated. Memory is encoding.

Your goal here: anchor. Tell stories, show outcomes, pause for impact.

"This one dashboard saved our last client 15 hours a week. That's someone's part-time job—gone."

Each layer demands different tactics. In the next section, we'll dive into the brain mechanics of attention—and how to align your demo with what the mind is wired to notice.

Section 3: How Attention Works in the Brain

The mind isn't passive—it's scanning, filtering, and deciding what's worth noticing.

Every second of your demo, the buyer's brain is doing triage. Out of the thousands of stimuli coming at them—your voice, your slides, their email pings, background noise—it's selecting what to focus on and what to discard. This filtering system is called the reticular activating system (RAS), and it's your biggest obstacle—or your biggest ally.

The RAS acts like a gatekeeper. It constantly asks:

"Is this relevant? Is this different? Is this emotionally important?"

If the answer is no, your demo content never even makes it to conscious thought. It gets dumped before the buyer's mind fully engages. That's why designing for attention isn't optional—it's biological.

How to Trigger the Brain's Attention Filters:

The brain pays attention to:

1. Novelty – Anything unexpected or different

"Most teams don't even realize they're losing time here..."

2. Contrast – Visual or verbal shifts

Use screen transitions, zooms, or "before and after" statements

3. Emotion – Especially surprise, urgency, or recognition

"Let me show you where most implementations fail—before ours kicks in."

4. Relevance – Direct connection to the buyer's world

"This ties directly to the metric you mentioned at the start of the call."

What the Brain Ignores:

- Predictable slide decks
- Long, flat monologues
- Screens without focal points
- Jargon without context

You're either triggering the RAS—or being filtered out.

Up next, we'll explore how to control visual attention on screen—so your demo shows what matters, not just everything available.

Section 4: Visual Attention—Designing with Focus in Mind

If everything is visible, nothing is remembered.

One of the biggest mistakes in software demos is showing too much, too soon. Complex dashboards, full-page menus, and cluttered interfaces may look impressive—but to the brain, they're noise. Visual overload fragments attention and increases cognitive load, leaving your buyer unsure where to look or what matters. That's why high-impact demos are designed not just to display software—but to guide visual focus. The goal isn't to show everything. It's to control what the buyer sees, in what order, and for what purpose.

Strategies to Guide Visual Attention:

1. Start with Framing Statements

   Before revealing a screen, tell them what to look for.

"This dashboard answers two critical questions—let me walk you through each one."

2. Zoom In, Not Out

   Use browser zoom or screen magnification to isolate key sections.

Show just the chart, not the full workspace.

3. Use Annotations or Mouse Movement

   Don't assume they're following your cursor—be deliberate.

Circle, highlight, or hover with intention.

4. Reveal Information Sequentially

   Hide non-essential menus or data until needed.

"I'll open this tab in a second—but first, notice what happens here."

Why This Works:
The brain can only consciously attend to one focal point at a time. When you guide that focus, you reduce mental effort—and increase clarity.
Visual control is memory control. What the eye sees with clarity, the mind remembers with ease.
In the next section, we'll shift from the screen to your spoken delivery, exploring how your voice manages auditory attention.

Section 5: Verbal Attention—How to Talk So They Stay With You
Your voice is not just a delivery tool—it's a focus tool.

Visual design helps guide the eyes—but your voice guides the brain. In a demo, your vocal presence determines whether your buyer tunes in—or tunes out. Monotone narration fades into background noise. But dynamic, intentional speech acts like a spotlight, signaling what matters and when to pay closer attention. Great demo presenters use their voice to manage attention rhythm—drawing buyers in, slowing down for key ideas, and injecting energy where needed.

Tactics for Verbal Attention Control:

1. Vocal Framing

   Cue the audience with phrases that signal importance.

"This next screen is where most teams go wrong—so watch closely."

2. Strategic Pauses

   Silence commands attention. Use it before or after key statements.

"That's right... the entire approval chain—automated."

3. Tone Variation

   Shift tone to signal changes in idea or emphasis.

   o   Lower tone = seriousness, importance

   o   Brighter tone = enthusiasm, discovery

"And here's where it gets interesting..."

4. Pacing Control

   Don't rush. Let key moments breathe. Match your speed to the content's complexity.

Complex workflows = slow, deliberate

Simple reveals = quick, confident

What to Avoid:

- Filler words ("basically," "just," "kind of") weaken clarity
- Rambling dilutes attention
- Speaking over screen changes confuses focus

The way you speak determines how—and whether—your message lands. Think of your voice as the auditory UI of your demo.

Up next: how to insert mental breathers that reset attention and prevent fatigue.

Section 6: Attentional Breaks and Mental Breathers

Because even great content needs room to breathe.

No matter how polished or relevant your demo is, your buyer's attention is still limited by biology. The brain needs periodic resets to stay alert, process information, and build memory. Without these breaks, even the best demos blur together, and cognitive fatigue quietly takes over.

That's where attentional breaks come in—brief pauses in content delivery that act as mental breathers. They don't slow down the demo; they energize it, giving the brain space to reset before moving on.

What Makes a Good Mental Breather?

1. Micro-stories or anecdotes

"Let me give you a quick example of how one client used this."

2. Mini recaps or signposts

"So far we've covered intake and routing—next, let's look at resolution paths."

3. Small questions or engagement cues

"Does this look similar to how your team handles it now?"

4. Humor or lightness (appropriately)

"No more Monday morning spreadsheet gymnastics."

The Science Behind It:

Mental breathers reduce cognitive load by creating:

- A shift in rhythm
- A moment of emotional reset
- An opportunity to encode the last chunk of information

Research shows that people retain more when learning is interrupted at the right intervals—not nonstop.

The Demo Rhythm Rule:

For most demos, plan a light reset every 3 to 5 minutes. Don't wait until the end to check in—check in along the way.

Attention is a finite resource. These resets extend its life.

Next, we'll cover what to do when attention slips anyway—and how to bring it back without losing momentum.

Section 7: Reclaiming Attention When It's Lost

Because drift happens—and great presenters know how to respond.

Even with the best delivery, buyers will drift. Cameras go off. Eyes drop. Someone starts replying to emails mid-demo. Don't take it personally. Attention lapses are part of the digital landscape. What matters isn't preventing every lapse—it's knowing how to pull attention back in without calling it out.

Great demo presenters recognize the signals of mental departure—and respond with subtle, respectful re-engagement tactics.

Signs That Attention Is Slipping:
- Delayed responses to questions
- Body language changes (camera off, posture slumps)
- Eyes darting to other screens
- Lack of questions or chat activity
- Repeated requests to "go back a slide"

Don't assume disinterest—assume cognitive fatigue or distraction.

How to Reclaim Attention Gracefully:
1. Use an "emotional re-hook"

"Let me show you the part that usually surprises people."

2. Shift the visual or narrative focus

Change screens, tell a story, or introduce a contrast.

"This next part flips the usual workflow on its head."

3. Ask a light-touch check-in question

"Would this help your onboarding team too?"

(Open-ended, not confrontational.)

4. Make it about them again

"Based on what you said earlier, I think this next feature is right in your wheelhouse."

What Not to Do:
- Don't call someone out for being quiet
- Don't double down on slides or features
- Don't rush or panic—stay steady, inviting, and adaptive

You're not losing the deal—you're just steering attention back onto the road.

Next, we'll tackle how to manage attention across multi-stakeholder demos, where competing interests can fragment focus even faster.

Section 8: Managing Group Attention in Multi-Stakeholder Demos

One screen. Five minds. Infinite distractions.

Multi-stakeholder demos are some of the most common—and most challenging—sales scenarios. You're not just speaking to one buyer with a singular need. You're speaking to a roomful of roles, each with different priorities, pain points, and levels of engagement.

Without careful design, attention splinters. The product lead is focused on features. The CFO wants cost savings. The operations lead wants workflow clarity. If your demo doesn't offer clear handholds for each, you risk losing all.

How Group Attention Works:
Group dynamics create pressure. People defer to loud voices or tune out when the content doesn't feel relevant. Attention doesn't scale automatically—you have to re-earn it from each participant.

Strategies for Managing Group Attention:

1. Stakeholder Signposting

"This next view will matter most to your finance and leadership teams."

2. Persona Rotation

Alternate your focus. Don't stay locked on one stakeholder.

"From a security standpoint, this part will be key. From a user experience perspective, let me show you what it feels like to log in day one."

3. Callbacks to earlier input

"Like you mentioned, Lisa, intake routing has been a big bottleneck—this screen addresses that directly."

4. Value Framing Across Roles

Tie one feature to multiple needs.

"This dashboard cuts workload for your staff, improves reporting for finance, and reduces errors for compliance."

Group Attention = Personalized Relevance:

You don't need to impress everyone at once—you need to make each person feel seen during the flow of your demo.

Up next, we'll explore how your tools and tech choices either support—or sabotage—that focus.

Section 9: Tools and Technology That Aid or Erode Attention

Tech can enhance focus—or quietly destroy it.

The tools you use during a demo are supposed to support your message. But too often, they become the main source of distraction. Clunky transitions, disorganized tabs, slow load times, or tool-switching gymnastics can derail buyer focus in seconds. To maintain attention, your tech stack must be invisible in its smoothness—helping guide attention without calling attention to itself.

Technology That Enhances Attention:

1. Annotation Tools

    Highlight, circle, or point to key areas in real time.

Tools like Zoom's Annotate, Microsoft Ink, or overlays help direct focus instantly.

2. Screen Framing Tools

    Use plugins or built-in browser zoom to simplify views.

141

Show one element at a time—less clutter = more clarity.

   3.   Cameras & Layouts

      A presenter-visible layout (side-by-side view) improves connection.

When they can see your face, empathy and trust increase.

   4.   Custom Environments

      Pre-set demo flows in sandbox environments prevent loading delays or broken sequences.

A clean flow builds confidence and reduces mental drift.

Technology That Breaks Focus:

- Tool overload: Switching between six windows or apps mid-demo
- Tab clutter: Dozens of visible browser tabs signal disorganization
- Disruptive alerts: Desktop notifications mid-demo break immersion
- Fumbling with login screens or permissions: Breaks flow and credibility

Pro Tip: Practice the Transitions:

Smooth transitions between tools, screens, and tabs is what separates amateurs from pros. Practice the flow. Time the steps. Cut what clutters.

Tech should be a silent partner in focus—not a competitor for it.

Up next: the Attention-Optimized Demo Framework—a repeatable structure to maintain engagement from start to finish.

Section 10: The Attention-Optimized Demo Framework

A repeatable rhythm to keep minds focused and memory active.

By now, you've seen that attention isn't something you get once—it's something you manage continuously. This section puts it all together in a structured, time-aware demo framework designed to maximize attention, reduce fatigue, and anchor memory across a standard 30- to 45-minute presentation.

Think of this as the mental pacing plan for your buyer's brain.

The 30-Minute Attention Framework:

Each phase includes a primary attention goal:

1. Minutes 0–3: The Hook
   o Emotional trigger, problem statement, audience relevance
   o Goal: Capture surface attention
2. Minutes 4–8: First Win
   o Quick payoff feature or time-saving insight
   o Goal: Move to sustained attention with surprise or relief
3. Minutes 9–14: Core Workflow

- o   Chunked walkthrough of your product's primary job
- o   Goal: Support understanding without overload
- o   Insert Attentional Breather #1 (story, recap, or light engagement)

4. Minutes 15–20: Personalization Pivot
- o   Tie product benefits to buyer-specific roles or data
- o   Goal: Create deep attention through empathy and relevance

5. Minutes 21–26: Aha Moment
- o   Show a transformational insight or emotional peak
- o   Goal: Anchor memory and commitment

6. Minutes 27–30: Close and Direction
- o   Recap key outcomes, next steps, emotional resolution
- o   Goal: End with clarity, confidence, and energy

Why It Works:

This structure mirrors how attention rises, dips, and resets. It gives the brain breathing room without losing momentum. And it helps you stay in control—no matter who's in the room or how complex the product.

You now have a full toolbox for managing attention. In the next chapter, we'll explore designing demos for memory—because what buyers remember is what drives what they do.

Chapter 9: Designing for Memory

What buyers remember determines what they do.

Section 1: Memory Is the Real ROI

Your demo isn't just being watched—it's being remembered, retold, and reinterpreted.

The real test of your demo doesn't happen during the call. It happens after—when the buyer logs off, joins their next meeting, and eventually has to explain your solution to someone else. At that point, what matters isn't what you said—it's what they remember.

And here's the hard truth: Most demos aren't memorable. They're clear, competent, even polished—but days later, they blur into a vague impression: "It seemed solid, I think... Something about automation?"

That's why designing for memory, not just delivery, is the secret weapon of high-performing sales teams. Because memory drives decision-making.

From Demo to Recall to Decision:

Memory is the real return on investment for every demo minute. If your message isn't sticky—if it can't survive the gap between the demo and the decision—you're not competing with better software. You're competing with better recall.

Think about what happens post-demo:

- Your buyer goes into a debrief with other stakeholders.
- They recap your product without your slides.

- They decide whether to bring you to the next stage.

If your demo wasn't designed with recall in mind, your champion becomes a weak proxy. They forget specifics, stumble over the pitch, or misrepresent the value. Not because they didn't care—but because they weren't set up to remember and retell.

From this point forward, your demos aren't just experiences. They're memory construction zones.

In the next section, we'll unpack how memory actually works—so we can design each part of the demo to stick where it matters most.

Section 2: How Memory Actually Works

You can't control what buyers remember—unless you design for how memory works.

Most demo presenters assume memory is automatic: "If I explain it clearly, they'll remember it." But the brain isn't a hard drive—it's a filter. Most of what you say is discarded within minutes unless it's encoded properly.

To design memorable demos, you need to understand the three stages of memory:

1. Encoding

This is the moment your message enters the brain. It's most effective when:

- The information is new and relevant
- It's tied to an emotion, image, or metaphor
- It's delivered at a moment of focus

If the buyer's distracted or overloaded, encoding fails—no matter how good the content.

2. Storage

This is where the brain decides what to keep. The brain favors:

- Emotionally charged content
- Concepts tied to existing knowledge
- Repeated or reinforced ideas

Without reinforcement, most demo content fades within hours.

3. Retrieval

This is the "test" moment—when the buyer tries to remember what you said. Retrieval is strongest when:

- The message was clearly structured
- Cues were embedded (visual, verbal, emotional)
- The buyer used the information shortly after learning it (e.g., in a recap meeting)

The Demo Danger Zone:

Most demos are clear at encoding... but weak in storage and retrieval. They're interesting in the moment—but not repeatable or recallable.

That's where cognitive design comes in.

In the next section, we'll apply this science to one of the most powerful rules in memory-based demos: the Rule of One.

Section 3: The Rule of One

One message per moment. That's all the brain can carry.

When it comes to memory, less is more—not because your buyer lacks intelligence, but because the brain has limits. The more ideas you cram into a single moment, the more you dilute all of them. The brain's working memory—its temporary "holding tank" for new information—can only process a handful of items at a time.

Enter the Rule of One:

Deliver one clear idea per screen, per explanation, per moment.

It's not just about simplicity. It's about cognitive respect.

Why the Rule Works:

- Clarity improves encoding
  When buyers know exactly what they're supposed to take away, they remember it.

"This screen cuts ticket triage time in half. That's the point."

- Focus drives retention

  One idea, delivered well, has a chance to stick. Three ideas blur together.

- Repetition becomes possible

  When messages are clean and singular, they're easier to repeat—especially by your internal champion.

Common Violations:

- Showing a full dashboard and explaining five things at once
- Delivering a rapid-fire list of features with no emotional anchor
- Using bullets instead of focusing on a verbal moment of meaning

Use the Rule of One in Practice:

- Frame every screen or slide with a single takeaway
- Ask: "If they only remembered one thing from this part, what would it be?"
- Deliver that thing with intention—and then stop talking

You're not minimizing your product. You're maximizing its memorability.

Next, we'll explore how to amplify those singular ideas using visual, verbal, and emotional memory hooks.

Section 4: Memory Hooks—Visual, Verbal, and Emotional

Want your demo to be remembered? Give the brain something to hang onto.

Most of what you show in a demo won't be remembered word-for-word. But certain moments will stick—because they're anchored to something the brain recognizes as important. These anchors are called memory hooks. They're small, intentional elements that give the mind a place to store and retrieve your message later.
There are three main types: visual, verbal, and emotional.

Visual Hooks:
The brain processes images 60,000 times faster than text.

- Use a single visual metaphor or simplified screen to tie a complex idea to an image.
- Highlight or zoom into what matters—isolate, don't decorate.

"Think of this dashboard like your mission control—everything flows through here."

Verbal Hooks:
The right phrasing becomes repeatable.

- Use alliteration, rhythm, or contrast to make key points stick.
- Repeat key phrases two or three times during the demo.

"Faster routing. Fewer tickets. Happier teams."

Emotional Hooks:

Emotions encode memory. A moment of relief, surprise, or pride becomes sticky.

- Tell a micro-story with stakes and resolution.
- Reflect the buyer's pain, then show transformation.

"One of our clients had 3,000 backlogged requests. They cleared it in 6 weeks—with this."

Stack the Hooks:

The most memorable moments combine all three:

- A visual cue
- A strong phrase
- An emotional insight

Your buyer may forget the full workflow—but they'll remember the feeling of clarity you created.

Next, we'll explore how to turn those hooks into full-blown sticky moments that anchor your entire demo.

Section 5: Creating Sticky Moments in Your Demo

One unforgettable moment can carry the whole message.

In every standout demo, there's a moment the buyer remembers days later. A single screen, phrase, or story that sticks in their mind—and becomes the reason they say, *"That's the one."* These aren't accidents. They're designed. We call them sticky moments—deliberate moments engineered for emotional and cognitive impact.

What Makes a Moment Sticky?

1. Surprise

   The moment interrupts expectation.

"Wait, it already sorted those requests?"

2. Relevance

   The buyer sees themselves in the story.

"That's exactly what our support team deals with every Monday."

3. Simplicity

   The message is clear, visual, and easily repeatable.

"Three clicks. Ten minutes. Done."

4. Emotion

   Relief. Excitement. Even humor. Any feeling that opens a memory loop.

"This used to take 40 hours a month. Now it takes one."

How to Create One in Your Demo:

- Identify a moment of transformation in the product: a before/after, manual-to-automated, complicated-to-simple switch.
- Add an emotional frame: describe what that change *feels* like to the user.

- Anchor it with a clear phrase: "This is the moment we call 'zero inbox mode.'"
- Then pause—let the moment land.

Sticky moments create demo recall gravity. Even if your buyer forgets 80% of the flow, that one high-impact point becomes the story they tell.

In the next section, we'll explore how to reinforce those moments through spaced recall—so they don't just stick now, but resurface when decisions are made later.

Section 6: The Science of Spaced Recall

You don't need to repeat everything—just the right things, at the right time.

Memory fades fast. Within an hour of your demo, your buyer will forget over 50% of what they saw. Within a day, up to 80% may be gone—unless you strategically reinforce it. That's where the science of spaced recall comes in.

Spaced recall is the practice of revisiting key information at intervals—not just repeating it, but helping the brain retrieve it. Every time you bring a key point back into focus, it becomes more stable in long-term memory.

How to Apply Spaced Recall in a Demo:

1. Revisit the key message mid-demo

155

"Remember how we started with that backlog problem? Watch how this automation resolves it in seconds."

2. Use verbal bookends

Introduce an idea early. Circle back to it later in a different context.

3. Call back to sticky moments

"This is where 'zero inbox mode' becomes reality."

4. Pause to summarize chunks

"So far we've seen three key shifts: visibility, automation, and routing speed."

These small, intentional repetitions tell the brain:

"This matters. Keep it."

After the Demo: Extend the Recall:

Spaced recall doesn't stop at the end of the call.

- Use follow-up emails to reference the sticky moment.
- Include recap visuals or one-slide summaries.
- Encourage internal retelling with ready-made phrases and benefits.

You're not being redundant—you're being memorable by design.

In the next section, we'll explore how to turn your demo into a story your buyer can *retell internally*—and why that's essential for moving deals forward.

Section 7: How Memory Shapes Internal Buy-In

You're not just demoing for the person in front of you—you're equipping them to sell for you.

After your demo ends, the decision-making journey is just beginning. Your champion now enters a gauntlet of internal discussions, recap meetings, and budget reviews. You won't be in the room—but your message will.

The problem? Most champions aren't trained to sell. If your demo didn't equip them with clear, recallable takeaways, they'll fumble the pitch, dilute the value, or default to vague enthusiasm:

"It looked good. I think it could help... but I'd have to check my notes."

That's why your real audience isn't just the buyer on the call—it's the room they walk into next.

Memory Fuels Advocacy:

A champion becomes effective when they:

- Remember your key differentiators
- Can explain your product in one or two sharp phrases
- Feel emotionally committed to the problem and solution
- Can defend the purchase internally without you

This doesn't happen by accident. It happens when your demo is retellable.

How to Make Your Demo Retellable:

1. Build a narrative arc: problem, solution, outcome

"They were drowning in manual tasks. Now they've cut processing time by 70%."

2. Offer repeatable phrases

"It's three clicks instead of thirty."

"One screen. All the data. No delays."

3. Give a takeaway deck or 1-page summary

Equip them with visual and verbal hooks that echo your demo's best moments.

You're not just delivering a message—you're training a messenger. In the final section of this chapter, we'll give you a simple tool to test how memorable your demo actually is: The Memorability Audit.

Section 8: The Memorability Audit

If your demo disappeared tomorrow, what would your buyer remember?

Most demo teams assess performance by asking:

"Did we explain it clearly?"

But clarity isn't the same as memorability. The better question is:

"What will they recall, repeat, and act on a week from now?"

To build a demo that closes deals, you need a feedback loop—and that starts with a memorability audit. This isn't a post-mortem. It's a design tool to build demos that stick from the start.

Ask These Questions After Every Demo:

1. What would the buyer say if asked, "What's the main benefit?"

   (If it's vague, your message wasn't sticky.)

2. Could they describe a key moment or metaphor?

   (Sticky moments matter more than walkthroughs.)

3. Was there a clear, emotional before-and-after story?

   (Memory loves transformation.)

4. Would they be able to sell it to their boss tomorrow?

   (If not, they won't push the deal forward.)

5. Did we reinforce the message through recall, repetition, and relevance?

Do a 24-Hour Check:

After the demo, ask yourself:

- If I couldn't use slides, how would I explain what we showed?
- Could the buyer do the same?

This exercise exposes the true clarity and durability of your message.

Pro Tip: Ask the Buyer:

End every call with:

"What stood out the most?"

You'll learn what landed—and what didn't.

The more memorable your demo, the more likely it drives action.

With attention and memory under your belt, the next chapter explores the final frontier: engagement—how to turn passive viewers into active participants.

Chapter 10: Designing for Engagement

Because the opposite of engagement isn't hostility—it's indifference.

Too many demos treat engagement as a lucky bonus—something that happens if the buyer feels especially curious. But engagement is designable. This chapter teaches how to shift your demo from a one-way broadcast to a two-way experience that activates interest, deepens understanding, and builds commitment.

Section 1: Why Engagement Is Essential in Modern Demos
Because attention isn't enough—your buyer needs to be involved.

You can have a clear message, a polished platform, and a beautiful screen—but if your buyer is just nodding along silently, you're losing ground. In today's selling environment, passive demos are forgotten demos. Engagement is what turns a passive observer into an active participant. And active participants become invested decision-makers.

Engagement isn't a bonus—it's the activation switch for everything else you've worked to build.

Engagement vs. Attention:

Attention means the buyer is watching. Engagement means they're processing, reacting, and making meaning in real time. It's the difference between someone nodding politely and someone interrupting with:
"Wait—could we use this for onboarding, too?"
That interruption? It's gold. It means they've moved from watching your story to placing themselves inside it.

Why Low Engagement Kills Demos:

When buyers don't engage:
- They retain less

- They surface fewer objections (so you never get to resolve them)
- They feel no ownership over the solution
- They struggle to advocate for you internally

You may think you're making great progress—when really, the deal is already drifting.

Why Engagement Wins:
Engaged buyers:
- Remember more (active processing boosts memory)
- Reveal more (giving you better discovery mid-demo)
- Buy in faster (emotionally and cognitively)
- Fight for you internally (because they co-created the value)

Your job isn't to impress them. Your job is to involve them. In the next section, we'll break down the Engagement Spectrum—and how to move buyers from passive to interactive.

Section 2: The Engagement Spectrum
Engagement isn't binary—it's a progression.

Most presenters think of engagement as either "on" or "off." But in reality, buyer engagement flows across a spectrum. You're rarely starting at zero, and you're rarely at full throttle. The goal isn't to "make it exciting"—it's to advance engagement, one level at a time.
Let's break it down into three levels, each with specific cues and tactics.

Level 1: Passive Engagement:
The buyer is watching, listening, maybe nodding—but not contributing.

Example: "Okay, yeah, I see how that works."

What to do here:
- Use attention hooks: a surprising stat, a bold claim, a key problem.
- Ask low-stakes check-ins: "Does this look familiar?"
- Add framing language: "This will be most relevant to your intake team."

Level 2: Reactive Engagement:
The buyer begins to respond, ask questions, or connect the dots.
Example: "Would this integrate with our ticketing system?"

What to do here:
- Validate and expand: "Yes—and let me show you how we've done that for others."
- Pivot into brief discovery: "What's your current process like?"
- Offer small choices: "Would you rather look at metrics or workflows next?"

Level 3: Interactive Engagement:
Now they're leaning in, offering scenarios, exploring implications.
Example: "Could this also replace our intake form system?"

What to do here:
- Invite collaboration: "Let's sketch out what that could look like."
- Tie directly to business outcomes: "That could save you 6–10 hours a week."
- Co-own the value: "Let's design this together."

Great demo presenters don't wait for interaction—they design for escalation. Next, we'll explore the cognitive triggers that drive each leap forward in engagement.

Section 3: Cognitive Triggers of Engagement
Engagement is emotional before it's logical.

Buyers don't engage because they "should." They engage because something in your demo sparks a response. Their brain flags the moment as novel, important, or rewarding—and that signal pulls them into participation. To create those signals, you need to trigger the brain's natural engagement drivers.
Here are four of the most powerful:

1. Novelty:
The brain is wired to notice what's new.
- Show something unexpected early: a dramatic time-saver, an unusual insight, or a fresh metaphor.

"Most teams don't know this, but 60% of their routing time is spent here."
Novelty wakes the brain up—and invites curiosity.

2. Relevance:
Engagement rises when buyers see themselves in the story.
- Use their language. Reflect their role.

"Here's how this would look for a billing coordinator like you."
The more personal the content feels, the deeper the engagement.

3. Autonomy:
People engage more when they feel in control.
- Offer small choices: "Do you want to look at metrics or user flow next?"

- Let them guide part of the path: "Want to test this scenario live?"

Autonomy turns the demo into a shared experience—not a performance.

4. Emotional Connection:
We act on what we feel.

- Highlight frustration, relief, or satisfaction.

"This is the moment most teams breathe a little easier."
Emotions encode engagement. Even subtle ones.

Great demos don't just show features. They create moments that matter to the brain.
In the next section, we'll look at one of the most overlooked engagement tools: asking better questions.

Section 4: Asking Better Questions During the Demo
Questions don't interrupt the demo—they are the demo.

Most demo presenters ask questions the way a waiter asks, "Still working on that?"—out of habit, not intention. But when used correctly, questions can ignite engagement, uncover objections, and personalize the value in real time.
The right question doesn't just gather information—it creates involvement.

What to Avoid:
- "Does that make sense?" (Assumes confusion)
- "Any questions?" (Too open-ended and passive)
- "Are we good so far?" (Encourages a nod, not a conversation)

These questions tend to close doors instead of opening them.

Better Question Types:

    1.   Situational

"How do you currently manage this process?"

"What's the biggest friction point in your intake flow?"

    2.   Comparative

"How does this differ from what you're using now?"

"Which part of this workflow feels more intuitive?"

    3.   Forward-looking

"If you had this tomorrow, where would you start using it?"

"Who else on your team would benefit from this?"

    4.   Role-specific

"For you as the compliance lead, does this meet audit needs?"

"As a team manager, would this dashboard reduce check-ins?"

Pro Tip: Time Your Questions:

- Early questions = curiosity + context
- Mid-demo = clarification + calibration
- Late-stage = future vision + decision-making

Don't wait until the end. Weave questions throughout your narrative like stepping stones. Every great question moves the buyer deeper into the experience—and closer to owning the solution.

Up next, we'll explore how to turn engagement into co-creation, where the buyer helps shape the flow of the demo.

Section 5: Engagement Through Co-Creation

If they help build it, they're more likely to believe in it.

One of the most powerful forms of engagement is co-creation—inviting the buyer to shape the demo in real time. When buyers participate in directing the flow, applying features to their world, or even naming a problem you just solved, they move from observers to owners.

You stop demoing *at* them and start building *with* them.

Why Co-Creation Works:
- It activates autonomy, a key engagement driver
- It increases relevance by aligning content with real-world use
- It creates emotional investment—because they helped shape the solution

When buyers co-create, they're no longer watching a vendor pitch—they're imagining success with your product as their own.

Ways to Invite Co-Creation:
1. Path Selection

"Would you rather look at your intake flow or escalation path next?"

2. Persona Pivoting

"Want to walk through this as a team lead or an end user?"

3. Scenario Modeling

"Let's sketch out how this would look for your remote team."

4. Input Collection

"What's the field name your team uses for priority tags? Let's use that here."

5. Naming the Win

"How would your team describe this improvement if we rolled it out?"

Bonus Effect: Ownership:

When a buyer helps design the demo path, they become emotionally aligned with the solution. It's no longer your software—it's their tool, their story, their win.

In the next section, we'll explore how engagement also helps surface objections early—and why that's a good thing.

Section 6: Using Engagement to Surface Objections Early
Objections aren't barriers—they're invitations.

Many presenters dread objections, treating them as signs of resistance or failure. But in reality, objections are often the clearest signals of engagement. A buyer who challenges, questions, or raises concerns is mentally processing your product—and trying to fit it into their world.
That's exactly what you want.
The danger isn't an objection. The danger is silence—a passive buyer who offers no resistance because they've already checked out.

Why Objections Are Valuable:
- They reveal underlying priorities or concerns
- They give you a chance to customize or clarify
- They indicate the buyer is thinking ahead

An objection is a buyer saying, "I'm trying to make this work—but something doesn't fit yet."

How to Encourage Objection-Surfacing:
1. Normalize friction

"It's common for teams to wonder how this fits with their existing process—anything coming up for you?"
2. Ask specific resistance questions

"Where do you see pushback from your team on a change like this?"
"What's the part that feels most uncertain right now?"
3. Listen without defensiveness

- o   Validate the concern. Don't immediately counter it.
- o   Clarify, then tailor your response.
4. Use their objection as a pivot

"That's helpful to hear. Let me show you how we've addressed that with another client in your space."

Don't Chase Avoidance:
When buyers avoid engaging, it's not a win—it's a warning. Draw them out. Create psychological safety for disagreement as discovery.
In the next section, we'll explore the tools that support real-time participation, especially in virtual and hybrid demos.

Section 7: Tools That Enable Real-Time Participation
If you want buyers to engage, give them a reason—and a way—to participate.

You can design the most interactive demo script in the world, but if the tools you're using don't support real-time participation, you're stuck with a passive experience. Whether you're presenting in person, remotely, or in a hybrid setting, your technology stack must invite interaction.
Fortunately, small shifts in tooling can open big doors for engagement.

Engagement-Boosting Tools:
1. Live Annotation Tools

Use Zoom's Annotate, Microsoft Whiteboard, or browser overlays to spotlight key elements.
✓ Great for visually reinforcing talking points
✓ Allows spontaneous emphasis
2. Polls and Micro-Surveys

170

Ask for quick input mid-demo: "Which workflow is more painful—intake or triage?"

✓ Captures attention

✓ Personalizes the next segment

    3.   Guided Click-Through Environments

Let buyers take control of the mouse or walk through a sandbox flow.

✓ Turns passive watching into active doing

✓ Builds confidence in usability

    4.   Embedded Chat or Q&A Panels

Encourage reactions and side questions during the session.

✓ Keeps quieter stakeholders involved

✓ Surfaces hidden concerns

    5.   Interactive Slides or Cards

Tools like Prezi or Pitch let you jump non-linearly based on buyer choices.

✓ Supports co-creation

✓ Feels adaptive and dynamic

The Key: Use Tools with Purpose:

Don't overwhelm buyers with novelty. Every tool you introduce should serve a clear engagement function. Practice with your stack. Plan transitions. Smooth delivery builds trust.

In our final section, we'll pull it all together with a pacing guide: how often, how early, and how intentionally to engineer engagement from start to finish.

Section 8: Building a Demo Engagement Plan

If engagement is critical, don't leave it to chance.

Too many demos rely on hope: "Maybe the buyer will speak up." But the best presenters don't wait for engagement—they plan it. Every demo should include a structured engagement plan: a rhythm of prompts, pauses, and participation points mapped to the buyer's journey.

Think of it like blocking for a play. Every scene includes a moment for the audience to get involved—not just to stay awake, but to stay invested.

Start with Strategic Checkpoints:
Plan for engagement touchpoints every 4–5 minutes. Examples:
- A targeted question ("What's your current process here?")
- A visual action ("Let me highlight what most teams miss.")
- A co-creation moment ("Let's test this with your data model.")

These breaks reset attention, activate memory, and reduce overload.

Build an Engagement Map:
Before the demo:
- List the buyer roles and likely priorities
- Identify 3–5 planned engagement moments tied to those roles
- Prepare optional paths based on their responses
- Plan questions in advance—don't improvise under pressure

Vary Your Engagement Methods:
Don't rely on one tactic. Use a blend of:
- Questions
- Co-navigation
- Scenario testing

- Role-specific pivots
- Visual callouts

Mixing modes keeps engagement from becoming mechanical.

Engagement = Design + Delivery:
The more intentional your engagement plan, the more flexible your delivery can be. You'll respond better in the moment because you're anchored in structure.

With attention, memory, and engagement mastered, you're now equipped to deliver demos that are not only understood—but felt, remembered, and acted upon.

Chapter 11: Designing for Decision

Because your demo isn't just a story—it's a signal.

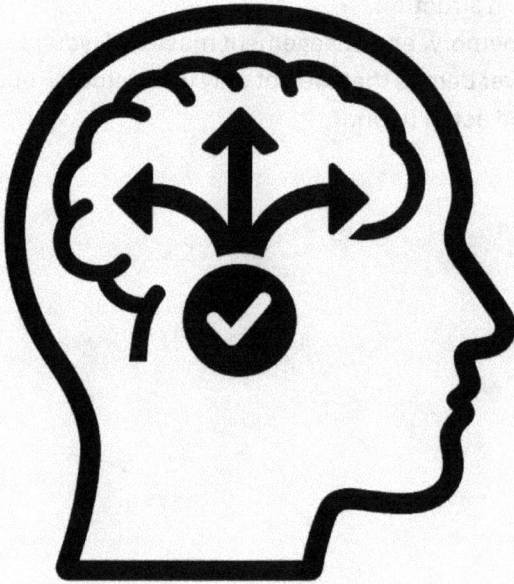

At some point, every great demo must shift from teaching to triggering action. Chapter 11 focuses on designing demos that inform and engage, and drive decisions by aligning with how the brain moves from consideration to commitment.

Section 1: Decisions Don't Happen in the Demo—But They Start There

The demo doesn't close the deal. It opens the mental doorway.

Every great demo ends with a sense of forward motion. But here's the truth: your buyer isn't going to make the final decision during your call. In most cases, the actual commitment happens days or weeks later, behind closed doors, under pressure, with competing priorities.

But what happens *during* the demo lays the psychological groundwork for that future moment.

Your goal isn't to get the contract signed in 45 minutes. Your goal is to create clarity, confidence, and momentum—so when it's time to decide, your solution feels like the obvious path forward.

From Insight to Intention

The demo should shift the buyer from curiosity to conviction:

- "This could work..." becomes → "We need this."

- "Let's explore more..." becomes → "Let's bring this to the team."

The buyer doesn't just need information—they need a feeling of certainty that the value is real, the risk is low, and the outcome is achievable.

That feeling starts in the demo.

The Decision Isn't Made—But It's Set in Motion:

You'll know you're on the right track when:

- The buyer starts using "we" instead of "you"

- They sketch next steps without being prompted

- They mentally rehearse their internal pitch to stakeholders

These aren't formal commitments—they're cognitive ones. And they're powerful predictors of deal velocity.

In the next section, we'll unpack how the brain actually makes decisions—and how to align your demo with the psychological processes that turn interest into action.

Section 2: The Neuroscience of Decision-Making

Decisions aren't made by spreadsheets—they're made by brains under pressure.

At its core, every buying decision is a neurological event. While we like to believe decisions are rational and calculated, research shows that emotion drives the engine, and logic justifies the route. Your demo doesn't just present a solution—it triggers a series of mental processes that lead to action... or hesitation.

Understanding these processes helps you design a demo that nudges the brain toward yes.

The Brain's Dual System: Emotion and Logic:

- The limbic system (emotional brain) responds first: *Do I like this? Does this feel right?*

- The prefrontal cortex (rational brain) follows: *Does this make sense? Is this a smart decision?*

If your demo doesn't first trigger emotional engagement—relief, curiosity, desire—it won't matter how logical your value proposition is.

The Approach-Avoidance Reflex:

Every decision involves a tug-of-war between:

- Approach: The promise of gain, ease, success

- Avoidance: The fear of cost, change, failure

Your job during the demo is to:

- Amplify approach signals (ease of use, speed, control)

- Minimize avoidance signals (complexity, risk, unknowns)

Each moment should whisper: *This is doable. This is safe. This is better.*

The Trust Loop:

Buyers loop through: *Understand → Trust → Imagine → Act*
If trust breaks at any stage—due to confusion, overload, or doubt—the loop resets.

Great demos reduce friction at each loop by reinforcing clarity, confidence, and emotional reward.

Next, we'll explore a major cause of broken trust and stalled decisions: The Cognitive Dissonance Trap.

Section 3: The Cognitive Dissonance Trap

Too much information creates hesitation, not confidence.

Cognitive dissonance is what happens when a buyer's brain can't reconcile what they're seeing with what they already believe, want, or understand. It's the internal tension that says, "This seems great, but... I'm not sure." In demos, dissonance is the silent killer of momentum.

And the most common cause? Too much complexity.

Overload vs. Clarity:

When we present too many features, options, or workflows, we assume we're proving value. But to the buyer's brain, we're creating a puzzle it didn't ask to solve. The reaction isn't excitement—it's anxiety. And anxiety leads to hesitation.

"I liked what I saw, but I need time to process."
(Translation: *I'm overwhelmed, and I don't want to make a mistake.*)

Signs You've Triggered Dissonance:

- Buyer stops asking questions and starts taking notes (trying to keep up)

- They delay committing to next steps ("We'll talk internally")

- They say things like "That's a lot to think about" or "We have to map this out"

None of these are hard no's. They're cognitive red flags: *Something doesn't quite fit.*

How to Reduce Dissonance in Your Demo:

- Use the Rule of One: one clear takeaway per segment

- Highlight transformation, not configuration

- Tie every feature back to an outcome, not a spec

- Pause for buyer reflection before layering more content

Your buyer's brain isn't asking for more proof—it's asking for more coherence.

In the next section, we'll look at how to shift from showing software to framing the buying outcome, which is what truly fuels decision-making.

Section 4: Framing the Buy vs. Showing the Tool

Your software is the vehicle. The buyer is buying the destination.

Most demo presenters focus on showing how the tool works. But buyers don't want a tour of your product—they want a preview of their new reality. That means your demo shouldn't just display functionality. It should frame the decision as a clear, compelling leap forward.

Don't just show the tool. Show what changes when they buy it.

Buyers Aren't Buying Features—They're Buying Outcomes:

Think about it from the buyer's perspective:

- They're not buying dashboards—they're buying insight
- They're not buying automation—they're buying time back
- They're not buying workflows—they're buying confidence in process

Your job is to translate product details into decision-ready value.

How to Frame the Buying Outcome:

1. Present the before/after contrast

"Right now, your agents manually escalate every ticket. With this, triage happens automatically in seconds."

2. Focus on what happens the day after implementation

"If you rolled this out tomorrow, your team could reduce backlog by 40% within a week."

3. Speak to tangible business impact

"This could save your ops team 12 hours a week—and reduce missed SLAs by 60%."

Shift Your Language:

Instead of:

"This screen lets you configure dynamic tags..."

Try:

"This is how your team avoids routing delays and keeps priority issues visible in real time."

By framing the buy, you help the buyer imagine what life after the decision looks like—and that's the first step to making it real.

Up next, we'll explore how to create decision cues that gently guide the buyer forward—without pressure or hard closes.

Section 5: Decision Cues You Can Engineer

Buyers don't need pressure—they need signals that it's safe to move forward.

A well-designed demo doesn't end with a dramatic close. It ends with subtle signals that guide the buyer from clarity to confidence to action. These are called decision cues—small, strategic elements that reduce uncertainty and make saying "yes" feel natural.

You're not forcing the decision. You're framing it as the next logical step.

The Psychology Behind It:

When buyers feel mentally prepared, emotionally secure, and cognitively clear, they are far more likely to commit. But the brain looks for evidence of momentum—not just features, but signals that others have made this decision and succeeded.

That's where your demo becomes more than a walkthrough. It becomes a permission structure for action.

Types of Decision Cues:

1. Social Proof

"Teams like yours at Acme Corp. and DeltaHealth moved forward after seeing this same use case."
✓ Creates confidence through peer validation

2. Momentum Framing

"Most buyers who get to this point schedule a pilot or team review within a few days."
✓ Signals a shared path forward

3. Option Anchoring

"You can explore this via a sandbox trial or go straight to a scoped pilot."
✓ Offers choice while nudging action

4. Ownership Language

"Here's how we'd recommend rolling this out with your current structure."
✓ Moves from general to specific—without pressure

These cues turn decision-making from a cliff into a bridge.

In the next section, we'll look at the ideal timing and tone for making the ask—without disrupting the emotional flow of the demo.

Section 6: Timing the Ask

There's a moment when the buyer is ready—don't miss it.

One of the most common mistakes in demo delivery is either rushing the close or avoiding it altogether. But the real skill lies in timing the ask—knowing when the buyer's cognitive and emotional readiness aligns. Ask too early, and you feel pushy. Ask too late, and the energy dissipates.

Buyers don't need a hard close. They need a well-timed invitation to move forward.

The Psychology of Timing:

The brain makes decisions best when it feels:

- Emotionally elevated (relief, excitement, confidence)

- Cognitively clear (knows what the next step is)

- Socially safe (doesn't feel manipulated or rushed)

That means the best time to ask isn't at the very end—it's at the peak moment of alignment, when:

- The buyer nods or expresses clear interest

- They ask forward-looking questions ("Could we roll this out by Q3?")

- They use inclusive language ("We'd want this to link with our system")

How to Time the Ask Naturally:

- Pause after a win: When you've shown something valuable, let it land. Then:

"Would it make sense to explore this in a pilot format?"

- Use momentum phrases:

"Next step from here is usually a stakeholder review or access to a sandbox."

- Anchor to their goal:

"You mentioned improving triage before year-end—would a trial this month help us stay on track?"

The best asks feel less like closing and more like continuing the motion you've already built.

In the next section, we'll create a framework for delivering a decision-ready summary that helps buyers commit with clarity and confidence.

Section 7: Building a Decision-Ready Summary

Clarity isn't what you say—it's what they remember when the call ends.

The final minutes of your demo are more than a wrap-up. They're the bridge to the buying conversation your champion will have with others. If you close without a crisp, meaningful summary, your message will dissolve into a blur of screens and features.

A decision-ready summary doesn't just recap the demo—it translates it into a clear, compelling buying case.

What a Great Summary Includes:

1. The core problem

"You're spending 6–10 hours a week just routing tickets manually."

2. The demonstrated solution

"We showed how the rules engine automates triage with three configurable settings."

3. The business impact

"That cuts routing time by 80% and improves SLA compliance."

4. A next step

"Most teams at this stage either schedule a stakeholder review or begin a pilot."

The Psychology: Help Them Retell It:

Your champion needs to repeat your story—sometimes the same day, sometimes a week later. A clear, structured summary acts like mental scaffolding. It gives them confidence and consistency when you're not in the room.

"They're the team that showed us how to automate our intake process in three steps."

That's stickiness. That's influence.

Pro Tip: Create a One-Slide Value Map:

- Visual: Problem → Product → Outcome

- Use it during your summary and include it in follow-up

- Simple, repeatable, memorable

Your demo ends not with applause, but with clarity and confidence.

Up next: how to extend that clarity after the call with effective follow-up that nudges the decision forward.

Section 8: Post-Demo Follow-Up That Nudges Decisions

The demo is the spark. Follow-up is the fuel.

The most memorable demos still need reinforcement. After the call ends, your champion returns to a noisy inbox, competing priorities, and internal skeptics. Without timely, targeted follow-up, even the best demo fades into background noise.

Your goal post-demo isn't to repeat the message—it's to amplify the decision moment and keep momentum alive.

Why the Brain Needs Reinforcement:

Memory degrades rapidly after the initial experience. Within 24 hours, your buyer will forget much of the detail—unless you help them re-encode the message through:

- Emotional recall (reminding them how it felt)

- Visual cues (simple, sticky takeaways)

- Action paths (what to do next)

Follow-Up That Drives Action:

1. Send a 1-page Decision Summary

   o Recap the problem, what was shown, and the business value

   o Include one clear next step (e.g., "Pilot: 2 users, 14-day window")

2. Include a Visual Anchor

   o Use the "Value Map" from your summary slide

o   Helps your champion pitch internally

3. Personalize the Subject Line

"Your New Intake Workflow – Follow-Up + Next Step"
Stands out in inbox clutter

Reinforces ownership

4. Follow-Up Timing Matters

o   Send within 2 hours if possible

o   Reconnect in 2–3 days with a check-in or resource

"Here's a case study on a similar team's rollout."

Follow-up isn't about being persistent—it's about being predictable, helpful, and memorable.

When done well, it reactivates the emotional and logical signals from the demo—nudging the buyer from impressed to invested.

Chapter 12: The Multi-Brain Demo

One demo. Many minds. Multiple decision paths.

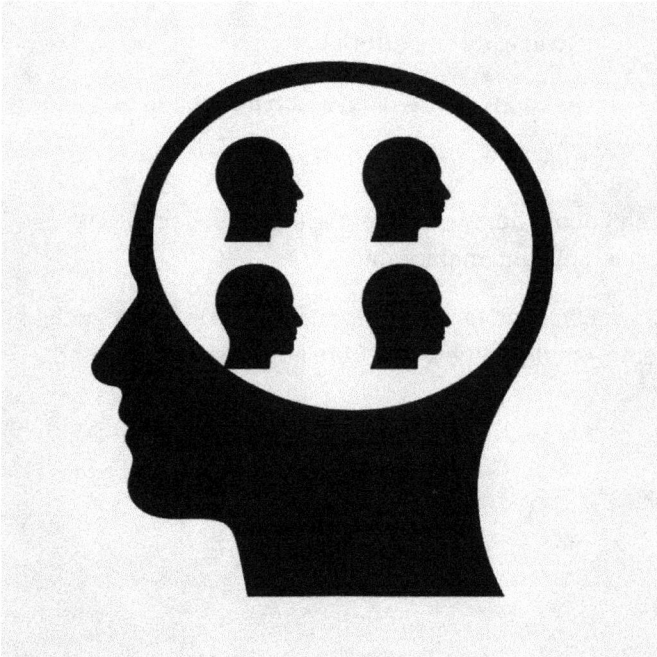

Selling to a team isn't just a bigger audience—it's a cognitive multiplier. Every person in the room brings their own goals, fears, learning style, and mental filter. A successful team demo doesn't treat the group as one mind. It respects the diversity of thinking—and designs for alignment.

This chapter explores how to demo effectively when your audience is a committee, not a contact.

Section 1: Why Group Demos Are Cognitively Complex

You're not just demoing to more people—you're demoing to more brains.

When you present to a group, you aren't scaling your message—you're multiplying the complexity. Each participant brings a unique blend of expectations, priorities, cognitive styles, and emotional filters. The result? Your demo now runs through a mental obstacle course of conflicting criteria, attention spans, and internal politics.

The danger isn't disagreement—it's disconnection.

The Multi-Brain Challenge:

Unlike one-on-one demos where you can read and adapt to a single person's cues, team demos force you to:

- Manage diverse mental models simultaneously

- Address conflicting goals without creating cognitive overload

- Keep everyone engaged—even those who never speak

In essence, you're demoing to a room full of different decision journeys—all happening at once.

The Risks of Treating the Room as One Mind:

- Tunnel vision: Focusing too heavily on one stakeholder's needs (usually the loudest)

- Misalignment: Assuming shared understanding when different people interpret value differently

- Silent sabotage: Unspoken concerns from secondary participants that stall deals post-demo

"The demo went great... but our compliance lead had concerns after the call."

Translation: *You demoed to one brain, but five others were in the room.*

The Goal: Cognitive Alignment, Not Uniformity:

You don't need everyone to love the same feature. You need each person to feel seen, and to recognize their piece of the win.

This section lays the groundwork for navigating group demos as a designed cognitive experience, not just a presentation.

Next, we'll identify the key stakeholders you're likely to encounter—and what each one needs to see, feel, and believe.

Section 2: Identifying Key Stakeholder Types

Different roles. Different brains. Different definitions of "value."

In any team demo, you're rarely selling to one decision-maker. You're selling to a coalition of influence—each person bringing their own lens on what matters. If you demo only to the power buyer, you risk losing the support of the people who make the solution work.

To design for alignment, you need to understand the cognitive goals of each stakeholder type.

Four Core Stakeholder Brains in a Buying Group:

1. Economic Buyer (The Investor Brain)

    o Focus: ROI, cost-benefit, time to value

    o Cares about: Outcomes, risk reduction, resource efficiency

    o Needs to hear: "This will pay for itself—here's how"

2. Technical Evaluator (The Engineer Brain)

    o Focus: Feasibility, integration, supportability

    o Cares about: Compatibility, architecture, compliance

    o Needs to see: "This fits into your existing stack securely"

3. Operational User (The Execution Brain)

    o Focus: Workflow, ease of use, time savings

    o Cares about: Daily experience, productivity, learning curve

- o Needs to feel: "This will actually make my job easier tomorrow"

4. Executive Sponsor (The Vision Brain)
   - o Focus: Strategic fit, brand alignment, cross-department impact
   - o Cares about: Big picture, transformation, leadership narrative
   - o Needs to believe: "This positions us for what's next"

Pro Tip: Stakeholder Stacking:

Sometimes, one person plays two or more roles. An ops lead might care about cost and workflow. A tech leader might wear the exec hat. Always listen for shifts in cognitive priority during the demo.

Up next, we'll look at how to frame the demo so it speaks to the whole room—without diluting its clarity.

Section 3: Framing the Demo for the Whole Room

One story. Many lenses.

When multiple stakeholders are in the room, the worst thing you can do is try to present everything to everyone all at once. That leads to diluted value, unclear focus, and cognitive overload. Instead, start by framing the demo as a shared journey with individualized meaning—a cohesive story that still allows each participant to see their own win.

Set a Unified Anchor:

Begin with a shared purpose that ties everyone together:

"Today we'll explore how you can reduce intake errors and improve resolution time—while staying aligned with your compliance and operational goals."

This primes the brain for goal-oriented processing and gives all parties a common destination—even if they care about different aspects of the trip.

Preview the Path:

Just like a tour guide, give a quick roadmap:

- What will be shown

- Who it's most relevant to

- Where they'll have opportunities to weigh in

"We'll start with how this supports frontline users, then pivot to technical integration, and finish with reporting outcomes."

This simple act reduces anxiety and gives each participant a reason to stay engaged, even when a segment doesn't directly apply to them.

Use Framing Language Throughout:

Reinforce shared value with inclusive phrasing:

- "From both a leadership and frontline perspective…"

- "For IT and ops alike, this step reduces time and touchpoints."

- "This is where finance and compliance typically align on value."

When you frame for the whole room, you turn parallel monologues into a collective conversation.

Next, we'll explore how to personalize the experience for each stakeholder—without derailing the demo's focus or flow.

Section 4: Personalizing Without Derailing

Tailor the moment—without losing the room.

One of the trickiest parts of a group demo is knowing when and how to personalize content. Go too narrow, and you risk alienating other stakeholders. Stay too broad, and no one feels seen. The sweet spot is lightweight personalization—quick, intentional adjustments that speak to individual roles without stalling the flow.

Why This Works:

The brain pays more attention when it hears something personally relevant. Even a simple callout can activate attention and emotional investment. But too much deep-diving into one person's world can trigger disengagement in others.

Personalization should feel like a glance, not a monologue.

Tactics for Focused Personalization:

1. Role-Based Asides

"From a billing perspective, this reduces code mismatches by 30%."
✓ Keeps the flow moving while acknowledging individual needs

2. Selective Deep-Dives (By Invitation)

"If it's useful, I can show how this connects to your audit log structure—want to go there now or later?"
✓ Respects time and prioritizes the group

    3.   Personal Language in Transitions

"For your team, Lisa, this part likely replaces a few manual steps, right?"
✓ Creates a moment of recognition without detour

    4.   Rotating Focus
       Intentionally alternate your attention:

- "From a tech lens..."

- "Operationally, what we see is..."

- "For finance leads, this often supports..."
  ✓ Keeps all parties engaged and valued

Remember: It's Still One Story:

You're customizing moments, not creating parallel demos. The key is to personalize with precision and pacing.

Next, we'll tackle how to manage the dynamics that arise when groups start talking, interrupting, or splitting focus.

Section 5: Managing Cross-Talk and Group Dynamics

You're not just presenting. You're facilitating a room of brains in motion.

In a team demo, attention is a fragile resource. A single sidebar, debate, or internal distraction can derail focus and fracture momentum. Group dynamics introduce variables: someone dominates, someone tunes out, someone starts a parallel conversation in the chat.

Your job is part presenter, part conductor—guiding attention while staying nimble.

Understand the Group Brain:

Group conversations aren't linear. One comment can create ripple effects:

- Shift focus away from the core message

- Trigger competing priorities

- Create confusion if stakeholders interpret differently

The solution isn't to control the room—it's to guide the energy.

Techniques to Manage Dynamics Smoothly:

1. Acknowledge and Redirect

"Great point. Let's bookmark that and loop back after this workflow segment—it connects nicely."

2. Use Names to Refocus

"That's helpful, John. I'd also love to hear Sarah's take—especially from an ops angle."

3. Control the Tempo

"Let's pause for 30 seconds—what's standing out to each of you so far?"
Regathers attention and encourages quiet voices

4.   Manage Chat and Sidebars Tactfully

"I saw a couple great points in the chat—let me bring those in."
Keeps everyone involved without splitting threads

5.   Signal Group Flow Intentionally

"Now let's shift lenses—from technical to executive view."
Prevents whiplash and clarifies transitions

The Real Skill: Attentional Leadership:

Buyers take cues from how you manage the room. Stay calm,
observant, and structured. Your ability to hold a group's attention
signals confidence, competence, and trustworthiness—all
essential to winning deals.

Next, we'll focus on how to guide the room toward shared
alignment and forward motion.

Section 6: Engineering Group Consensus

You can't force agreement—but you can guide it.

In multi-stakeholder demos, the real decision-making doesn't
happen during your call—it happens after, in conversations you're
not part of. Your mission? Equip the group to leave aligned. That
means using your demo not just to inform or impress, but to
engineer consensus through shared language, role-specific wins,
and inclusive moments.

Why Consensus is Tricky:

- Different roles = different priorities

- Internal politics may keep some voices quiet

- Without structured alignment, post-demo discussions become:

"I liked it." / "I didn't see the value." / "I'm not sure it fits our model."

Your job is to reduce fragmentation and increase agreement before the meeting ends.

Consensus-Building Tactics:

1. Verbal Alignment Checkpoints

"Does this workflow meet everyone's needs so far?"
Surfaces misalignment early

2. Summarize Shared Wins Out Loud

"So far, we've seen how this saves ops time, fits with IT's stack, and reduces reporting delays for finance."

3. Invite Silent Stakeholders In

"We've heard from tech and ops—does this also resonate from a compliance view?"

4. Use Language of Collective Ownership

"If your team rolls this out..."
"When you're managing these reports..."
Encourages "we" thinking

5. Create a 'Demo Consensus Slide'

   - A 1-slide visual showing 3–4 value points mapped to stakeholder roles o   Recap with: "Here's what we believe matters most to each of you."

When people leave a demo already agreeing on the value—even in broad strokes—they're more likely to support action later.

Let's now look at how to follow up with a group in a way that respects role differences while reinforcing alignment.

Section 7: The Post-Demo Debrief Plan

You don't just follow up—you follow up with precision.

After a group demo, your follow-up has to do more than recap what happened. It must speak to each stakeholder's brain, reinforce the aligned value story, and equip your champion to maintain momentum internally. Generic thank-you emails won't cut it.

You need a targeted debrief strategy that recognizes the multi-brain nature of the room—and keeps each one engaged.

Tailor Follow-Up by Role:

1.   Economic Buyer

     o   Focus: ROI, timeline, decision risk

     o   Asset: 1-page value summary with cost-benefit breakdown

     o   Message: "This reduces X by Y and pays for itself in Z months."

2.   Technical Stakeholder

- o Focus: Feasibility, stack fit

- o Asset: Architecture diagram, security FAQs

- o Message: "Here's how we integrate and comply with your standards."

3. Operational Users

- o Focus: Usability, daily impact

- o Asset: Screenshot walkthrough or short video clip

- o Message: "See how this step replaces your current manual process."

4. Executive Sponsor

- o Focus: Vision, transformation, strategic alignment

- o Asset: Narrative summary deck with org-wide outcomes

- o Message: "Here's how this supports your broader goals."

Reinforce Group Alignment:

Send a shared recap slide showing how each role's needs were addressed:

"This is what we covered—and how it maps to your team's priorities."

Include a clear call to action:

"Suggested next step: Stakeholder pilot or executive review meeting."

Pro Tip: Pre-Debrief the Champion:

Before you send anything group-wide, check in with your internal champion. Align your messaging with what *they* felt landed—and where resistance may linger.

With this, you close the loop not just on the demo, but on buying consensus.

Chapter 13: Memory Anchors

If they can't remember it, they can't buy it.

Even the most compelling demo will fade from memory unless it's structured to be sticky. Buyers are bombarded with messages, meetings, and competing pitches. This chapter explores how to use cognitive science and storytelling techniques to ensure your message isn't just heard—it's remembered, recalled, and repeated.

Section 1: Why Memory Matters More Than Mastery

They don't need to understand everything. They need to remember the right things.

It's tempting to think the goal of your demo is to fully educate the buyer—to walk them through every feature, explain every workflow, and cover every use case. But here's the reality: buying decisions aren't made based on total understanding. They're made based on what sticks after the demo ends.

In a world full of noise, complexity, and cognitive load, your buyer is trying to carry your message into rooms you'll never be invited into. If they can't remember the key value points, your demo might as well not have happened.

What the Brain Actually Keeps:

Cognitive science tells us:

- We remember moments, not monologues

- We retain emotionally charged content better than neutral information

- We forget 50–80% of new material within 24 hours—unless it's anchored

This means the actual content of your demo matters less than how memorable it is.

Shift the Goal: From Teaching to Triggering Recall:

You're not trying to make your buyer a subject-matter expert. You're giving them a set of mental hooks they can use to:

- Recall key benefits

- Explain them to others

- Advocate for the purchase with confidence

It's not "How much did they learn?"
It's "What did they walk away able to repeat?"

Your demo should be a memory experience—one that's easy to rehearse, retell, and rally behind.

In the next section, we'll look at how the brain's shortcut systems work—and how you can use those shortcuts to your advantage in every demo.

Section 2: The Brain's Shortcut System – How We Actually Remember

The brain is lazy. Use that to your advantage.

The human brain doesn't store everything it sees or hears. It compresses, simplifies, and files away only what it deems important, surprising, or emotionally resonant. This means your job in a demo isn't to deliver comprehensive information—it's to design for cognitive efficiency.

Understanding how the brain forms and retrieves memories allows you to shape a demo that's easier to remember—and harder to forget.

Three Key Memory Mechanisms:

1. Schema
    The brain connects new information to existing frameworks. If something fits into what we already understand, it sticks better.

"This works just like your current triage—but it's automated."
Leverages familiarity to create comfort and retention

2. Chunking
    Our working memory holds about 4–7 items at once. Grouping related concepts into "chunks" makes them easier to process and recall.

"Three things to remember: faster routing, fewer errors, and full visibility."
Breaks complex ideas into repeatable takeaways

3. Anchoring
    Vivid phrases, visuals, or metaphors "stick" when tied to a specific benefit or emotional cue.

"This is like having a traffic controller for your support queue."
Gives abstract ideas a physical or emotional anchor

Use the Brain's Shortcuts to Your Advantage:

Instead of overwhelming with detail, design your demo to:

- Fit into the buyer's mental model

- Group ideas into digestible sets

- Include distinctive anchors that are easy to recall and share

Next, we'll explore how to craft verbal anchors—memorable phrases that stay with your audience and become part of how they tell your story.

Section 3: Verbal Anchors – Sticky Phrases That Travel

What gets repeated gets remembered—and what gets remembered gets bought.

Your buyer won't replay the entire demo in their head. What they will do is recall a few key moments—and more importantly, repeat those moments to others. That's why you need verbal anchors: short, vivid, memorable phrases that distill your value into a soundbite that travels through the organization.

These phrases become the internal shorthand for why your product matters.

Why Verbal Anchors Work:

The brain is wired to retain:

- Rhythmic language

- Simple phrasing

- Emotionally or visually rich words

Think of how slogans work in advertising. A verbal anchor is a demo-specific slogan—a phrase your champion can repeat in a meeting or pitch deck.

"It's like auto-pilot for your approvals."
"Zero rework. Full audit. Always on."
"From chaos to clarity—in under 10 minutes a day."

How to Craft Great Anchors:

1. Use Contrast

"Manual in, automated out."
Highlights transformation

2. Use Numbers

"One click instead of five."
Feels concrete and efficient

3. Use Metaphor

"This is your mission control for onboarding."
Creates visual and emotional resonance

4. Use Repetition and Rhythm

"Fast to launch, easy to use, built to scale."
Increases retention and repeatability

Build These Into Your Script:

Don't wait for a clever phrase to appear mid-demo. Design your verbal anchors in advance and position them at emotional high points in your story.

In the next section, we'll pair words with visuals—creating powerful memory anchors your audience can both hear and see.

Section 4: Visual Anchors – Make It Seen and Remembered

What they see shapes what they remember.

In high-stakes demos, visuals aren't just decoration—they're cognitive cues. A well-designed visual can encode an idea in the buyer's brain faster and more permanently than words alone. But most demos rely on crowded screens, technical dashboards, or complex workflows—none of which stick.

To create visual anchors, you need to design single, unforgettable images that tell your story at a glance.

Why Visuals Stick:

- The brain processes visuals 60,000 times faster than text

- We retain 65% of visual content after three days—versus 10% of spoken content

- Memory improves when visuals are tied to emotion or contrast

In short, visuals make your message faster to absorb and harder to forget.

What Makes a Great Visual Anchor:

1. Simplicity

Use clean diagrams, not data dumps
Aim for a one-screen visual that captures the key idea

2. Contrast

Before/After, Old Way/New Way, Chaos/Clarity
Creates mental separation and emotional impact

3. Symbolic Representation

A stopwatch for speed, a checklist for confidence, a locked vault for compliance
Turns abstract benefits into recognizable icons

4. Alignment with Language

Pair visual with a verbal anchor:
Image: bottleneck funnel → Phrase: "From jammed to streamlined"
Reinforces memory through dual encoding

Where to Use Visual Anchors:

- Opening context slide (the problem)

- Transformation slide (the outcome)

- Recap slide (the value map)

Buyers won't recall every screen. But they will remember how it looked when it all made sense.

Next, we'll explore how to embed emotion into your demo—so your message doesn't just land, it lingers.

Section 5: Emotional Anchors – Tie Memory to Meaning

We don't remember facts. We remember how those facts made us feel.

Emotion is the accelerant of memory. No matter how logical your demo may seem, the most enduring moments are those that create emotional resonance—relief, excitement, pride, even fear of staying stuck. Buyers may justify with logic, but they decide based on feeling. To make your message unforgettable, you must tie value to emotion.

Why Emotion Enhances Memory:

The brain tags emotional experiences as important. That's evolutionary: feelings signal relevance and urgency.
When your demo evokes emotion, it tells the buyer's brain:

"This matters. Pay attention. Remember this."

Emotion also makes abstract benefits personal:

- Time savings becomes *peace of mind*

- Compliance becomes *sleeping better at night*

- Automation becomes *freedom to focus*

How to Build Emotional Anchors:

1. Surface Real Pain

"Right now, your team is losing 5 hours a week just chasing approvals."
Creates shared frustration and urgency

2. Paint the Future State

"Imagine your inbox on Monday—zero flagged items, full visibility."
Builds desire and emotional relief

3. Use Identity Language

"This is what modern finance teams are moving toward."
Appeals to personal and team identity

    4.   Name the Emotion

"That's the moment most clients say, 'Wow, that's a game-changer.'"
Gives buyers permission to feel—and remember

Emotional Anchors Make It Stickier and Shareable:

When buyers *feel* something during your demo, they're more likely to remember it, repeat it, and act on it.

Next, we'll close the loop with techniques for reinforcing all of these anchors—after the demo ends.

Section 6: Reinforcing Memory After the Demo

Repetition doesn't annoy the brain—it helps it remember.

Even the most well-anchored demo will fade unless you reinforce it. Memory isn't just created in the moment—it's strengthened in the days that follow. The best demo presenters don't just deliver great sessions. They deliver smart, structured follow-up that replays the right ideas using different formats and channels.

This is called the recap loop—and it's how memory becomes momentum.

How the Brain Strengthens Memory:

Neuroscience shows that memory consolidation happens through:

- Repetition (especially across formats)

- Contextual recall (seeing the same idea in a new way)

- Emotional reinforcement (linking new exposure to past impact)

That means you're not being redundant—you're being neurologically smart.

Build Your Memory Reinforcement Loop:

1. Email Recap (Day 0–1)

   o Key takeaways + verbal/visual anchors

   o Personalized by stakeholder

"Here's the workflow we discussed—cutting triage time by 80%"

2. Follow-Up Asset (Day 2–3)

   o PDF value map, video snippet, or annotated screenshot

"A quick visual of how your before/after looks in this setup"

3. Social Proof or Case Study (Day 4–5)

   o Connect their situation to a relatable win

"A team like yours went live in 12 days and reduced errors by 60%"

4. Next Step Prompt (Day 5–7)

   o Re-anchor the outcome and invite forward motion

"Let's explore what this would look like for your team next quarter"

Pro Tip: Build a "Memory Kit" for Champions:

Provide your internal champion with a few tools to retell your story:

- Slides, soundbites, and visuals

- Suggested phrases to explain key points

- Recap bullets tailored to their stakeholders

This closes Chapter 13 and sets the stage for the next shift: adapting the cognitive demo for remote and hybrid environments.

Chapter 14: Virtual Presence

You don't need to be in the room to command it.

Remote and hybrid demos are now the norm—but they come with new cognitive and emotional challenges. When you're not physically present, you lose access to critical cues: body language, eye contact, shared energy. This chapter shows you how to reclaim presence, project clarity, and anchor attention even across a screen.

Section 1: The Remote Attention Gap

When you're not in the room, attention leaks faster.

In a virtual demo, you're not just delivering content—you're competing with a thousand distractions. Email, Slack, calendar pings, kids, pets, fatigue. The environment isn't built for focus. And even if your demo is sharp, you're still operating through a screen that shrinks presence and divides attention.

The result? The buyer's cognitive load increases, but their ability to stay present decreases.

Why Remote Demos Strain Attention:

In physical rooms, attention is reinforced by:

- Body language

- Group energy

- Environmental cues (conference rooms signal "pay attention")

In virtual environments, those anchors vanish. Now:

- The brain can drift more easily

- There's no social pressure to stay engaged

- People can look attentive while mentally multitasking

What feels like a great delivery on your end may land as a blur of screens on theirs.

Signs of the Remote Attention Gap:

- Delayed responses or vague affirmations ("Makes sense...")

- Flat facial expressions or cameras off

- Fewer questions or comments compared to in-person demos

- Post-demo confusion about things you clearly covered

These aren't signs of disinterest—they're symptoms of cognitive disconnection.

The Goal: Hold Attention by Design, Not Force:

In remote demos, you don't "earn" attention—you engineer it. That means:

- Delivering in short, high-impact bursts

- Reinforcing key points through verbal and visual anchors

- Building in micro-interactions to re-engage drifting minds

The rest of this chapter will show you how to craft a remote experience that commands the room—even when you're not in it.

Section 2: Designing a Virtual Demo for Cognitive Flow

If attention is fragile, your structure needs to be bulletproof.

In virtual demos, the structure of your presentation becomes more important than ever. Without the grounding presence of a physical room, your buyer's brain is more likely to wander, fatigue, or disengage—even if your message is strong. The key to success is designing your demo with cognitive flow in mind: a deliberate rhythm of content, pauses, and cues that guides focus and prevents burnout.

Virtual Attention Rhythms Are Shorter:

Research shows that remote attention spans tend to reset or break every 4–7 minutes. That's the point where mental fatigue sets in and retention drops.
In a virtual setting, you can't afford long monologues or uninterrupted product walkthroughs.

Tactics to Create Cognitive Flow Remotely:

1. Segment Your Demo
    Break your story into tight, modular segments (4–5 minutes each)

Example: "First, let's look at how tickets get created. Then we'll pivot to routing logic."

Each segment resets attention and builds momentum

2. Use Verbal Transitions to Reset Focus

"Now let's shift to the part that finance leads usually care most about..."

Keeps the brain oriented and prepares for the next idea

3. Add Strategic Pauses

    o   Pause after key moments to let the message land

    o   Ask a quick check-in or pulse question

    Creates processing space and re-engagement

4. Use a Clear Start/Stop Loop
    Begin each section with what they'll see and end with what
    it means

"You just saw the auto-routing in action. That saves your team 2
hours a week."

Make Flow Feel Effortless:

A well-structured virtual demo should feel like a series of small
wins. Each moment builds clarity and keeps the audience with
you—without requiring them to fight for focus.

Section 3: Tools for Remote Engagement

You're not in the room, but your tools are.

When you demo virtually, you lose the nonverbal cues that help
gauge interest and guide pacing. What you gain, however, is a
toolkit of digital engagement options—chat, polls, annotation,
screen control—that, when used intentionally, can actually make
your session more interactive than in-person.

But here's the key: don't overuse them. Use them with purpose, not novelty.

Why Interactivity Matters Remotely:

The brain disengages faster when it's passive. Light engagement:

- Activates working memory

- Promotes information retention

- Signals the brain to pay attention to what happens next

Even small prompts can snap a drifting mind back into focus.

Tools and How to Use Them Strategically:

1. Chat Box

"What's your current workflow look like for this process?"
✓ Low-pressure way to create dialogue
✓ Great for quiet or camera-off audiences

2. Polls or Quick Reactions

"How confident are you in your current system—1 to 5?"
✓ Gives you instant feedback and prompts reflection

3. Annotations / Whiteboards

"Let's circle the part of this flow that costs the most time today."
✓ Makes abstract conversations tangible

4. Spotlight Moments

"John, from an IT standpoint, does this raise any red flags?"
✓ Encourages active listening and inclusive discussion

What to Avoid:

- Don't ask forced or generic questions just to be interactive

- Don't multitask with tools—use one at a time, clearly

Make Engagement Feel Natural:

Remote tools should feel like part of the conversation, not a gimmick. Used right, they help simulate presence and build trust.

Next, we'll explore how to project presence through your voice, face, and screen—without ever stepping into the room.

Section 4: Your On-Screen Presence

You don't need a stage to own the room—you just need the frame.

In virtual demos, your body may be offstage, but your face, voice, and screen become your entire presence. They are your only tools to signal credibility, energy, and confidence. This means your appearance, posture, and tone carry more cognitive weight than you might realize.

You're not just demoing a product—you're demoing you as someone buyers can trust.

Why Virtual Presence Matters:

Without in-person chemistry, the brain uses micro-signals to assess:

- Confidence: "Do they seem sure of this?"

- Competence: "Do they know what they're doing?"

- Warmth: "Do they seem like someone I'd want to work with?"

Strong virtual presence improves perceived value, retention, and likelihood to act.

How to Optimize On-Screen Presence:

1. Framing and Eye Line

   o Camera at eye level, centered frame

   o Look at the lens when speaking to simulate eye contact
   ✓ Builds connection and reduces perceived distance

2. Lighting and Clarity

   o Light your face from the front, not behind

   o Use a clean, non-distracting background
   ✓ Keeps focus on you, not your environment

3. Voice and Expression

   o Vary your tone and pacing; pause purposefully

   o Use natural facial expression and gestures
   ✓ Creates emotion and holds auditory attention

4. Posture and Movement

   o Sit forward slightly to convey engagement

   o Avoid fidgeting or looking off-screen

   o Signals control and focus

Use the "Warm Authority" Effect:

Aim for a tone that blends clarity and kindness: confident, composed, but never robotic. In remote demos, that mix builds both trust and attention.

Next, we'll explore how to design demo visuals that don't just look good—but work on any screen.

Section 5: Visual Design for Virtual Stickiness

If they can't see it clearly, they can't think about it clearly.

In virtual demos, visual clarity is everything. Your audience is likely viewing your content on a laptop—or worse, a phone. If your visuals are cluttered, text-heavy, or too small, the message gets lost. The cognitive burden increases, and attention drops.

That's why your visuals must be designed for digital digestion— built not for you, but for the brain on the other side of the screen.

The 3-Second Rule for Demo Slides:

Ask yourself:

"Can a viewer understand the point of this screen in 3 seconds?"

If the answer is no, you're asking them to work too hard. And in a remote setting, they simply won't.

Principles for High-Impact Virtual Visuals

1. Simplify Your Layouts

   o Limit each visual to one idea

o   Remove non-essential labels or background noise

✓ Keeps the viewer cognitively centered

2. Use Size and Contrast Intentionally

   o   Big fonts. High color contrast. No fine print.

   o   Make your key insight the most visually prominent thing

   o   Draws the eye exactly where you want it

3. Design for Mobile Viewing

   o   Avoid cramming data tables or dense dashboards

   o   Preview your slides on a phone if possible

   o   Ensures accessibility across all screen types

4. Pair Each Visual with Verbal Emphasis

"What you're seeing here is the single biggest time saver—auto-triage in action."

Locks in memory through dual-channel input

When in Doubt, Zoom In

Don't hesitate to zoom into one specific workflow step or value detail. Focus brings clarity—and clarity keeps attention.

Up next, we'll close the chapter with strategies for reinforcing your message after the virtual demo ends.

Section 6: Virtual Recap and Reinforcement

The demo ends. The buying process begins.

In virtual sales, the close of your demo isn't the finish line—it's the starting point of decision-making. Buyers are more likely to forget what they heard, misremember details, or struggle to explain the value to others. That's why your virtual demo must end with a deliberate recap and a follow-up strategy that reinforces your message across formats and moments.

When the buyer logs off, your message has to keep working—without you there to repeat it.

Why Recap Matters More Remotely:

- Remote demos are more prone to cognitive leakage

- There's often no hallway chat or post-demo debrief

- Champions must retell your story internally—often via email or slide

Your job is to equip them with the tools and language to do that well.

Virtual Recap Best Practices

1. End the Demo with a Verbal Summary

"Just to recap—we saw how this reduces intake time, integrates with your current system, and gives ops full visibility."

Re-engages short-term memory and signals closure

2. Send a Role-Based Follow-Up

o   Tailor your recap to each stakeholder's lens

"For finance: audit-ready tracking. For IT: low-lift deployment. For ops: 40% fewer escalations."

3. Use a Visual Recap Slide or Video Clip

o   Create a one-slide or 30-second summary of key benefits

o   Portable, replayable, and easy to share internally

4. Include the Next Step Clearly

"Would you like to explore a sandbox trial or map this to a pilot scenario?"

Make It Easy to Remember and Repeat

When your demo is over, your message should still be in motion—clear, sticky, and actionable.

Chapter 15: The Story Stack

One product. Multiple stories. One unforgettable experience.

Great demos don't just show features. They tell layered stories—
stories that speak to multiple roles, address emotional and
rational needs, and follow a clear narrative arc. This chapter
introduces the Story Stack: a multi-level storytelling framework
that lets you weave together context, pain, solution, and value
without overwhelming or fragmenting your audience.

Section 1: Why Stories Stick When Features Don't

The brain is wired for narrative—not product specs.

You've probably seen it happen: a buyer nods along during a
feature walkthrough, but can't explain why it matters 24 hours
later. That's because the brain doesn't remember information the
same way it remembers a story. Stories give facts meaning. They
organize data into patterns we understand. Most importantly, they
activate emotional and sensory parts of the brain—making your
message memorable, portable, and repeatable.

What Story Does to the Brain:
- Activates more brain regions than raw data (including
  sensory and emotional areas)
- Improves comprehension and recall by 2–5x
- Creates empathy and connection, making your buyer care,
  not just understand

In sales demos, stories transform your product from a set of
features into a solution with a purpose. They make your buyer the
hero—not just the audience.

Story Beats Stats Every Time:

Consider these two statements:
- "Our software routes tickets 27% faster using AI-based rules."
- "Imagine your team coming in Monday morning to find every ticket already assigned, prioritized, and halfway done."

Which one do you remember?

The second one turns data into experience. It shows, rather than tells. It engages imagination—and creates a future-state scenario the buyer wants to step into.

Why This Matters for Your Demo:

In a crowded market, features blur together. What buyers remember is how your solution made them feel:
- Understood
- Empowered
- Excited about a better way

Stories don't just convey information—they build belief. And belief is what moves deals forward.

In the next section, we'll break down how to layer these stories—strategically—throughout your demo using the Story Stack framework.

Section 2: The Layers of the Story Stack

Not all stories serve the same purpose—so stack them.

Your demo needs to resonate with different brains in the room: the executive who wants vision, the user who wants ease, the IT lead who wants feasibility. Each is looking for a story that speaks to their version of success. That's where the Story Stack comes in—a

228

layered narrative approach that lets you shift depth and focus without losing clarity or control.

The Three-Layer Story Stack:
1. Top Layer: The Vision Story
    o Why this matters now
    o The big picture of transformation
    o Ideal for executives and early-stage inspiration
2. Middle Layer: The Workflow Story
    o A relatable, human-centered use case
    o "A day in the life" narrative
    o Connects to end-users and operational leads
3. Base Layer: The Detail Story
    o The supporting data, configuration, or edge cases
    o Satisfies IT, legal, compliance, and procurement brains
    o Anchors the rest of the story in credibility

How the Stack Works:
- Start at the top, with vision.
- Drop to the middle, showing practical application.
- Dive to the base only when prompted or as needed.
- Climb back up to close on outcomes and value.

Think of it like an elevator. You can stop at any floor, but you always know which floor the buyer needs most.

Why Layering Wins:
With Story Stack, you never overload or underwhelm. You meet each audience where they are—without fragmenting your flow. It's flexible, scalable, and cognitively sound.

Up next: how to craft a Vision Story that inspires action and frames your entire demo.

Section 3: Crafting the Vision Story

If you don't frame the future, someone else will.

The Vision Story is your narrative north star. It's not about what your product does—it's about what the buyer could become because of it. This story sits at the top of the Story Stack and speaks to aspiration, transformation, and identity. It shows the buyer a world that's better, faster, or simpler—and positions your solution as the key to that world.

Why Vision Stories Work:
They tap into:

- Emotion: Buyers are more motivated by improvement than preservation
- Identity: People buy when it aligns with who they are or want to be
- Urgency: The "why now?" creates forward momentum

In a sea of feature comparisons, Vision Stories differentiate by inspiring action.

Elements of a Strong Vision Story:

1. The Before State
   o Describe their world today with clarity and empathy

"Right now, teams are stuck triaging issues manually—slow, error-prone, and invisible."

2. The Obstacle
   o Define what's holding them back

"Legacy systems weren't designed to adapt. They react—but they don't predict."

3. The Breakthrough
   o   Show how your product enables change
"What if your system could learn from every ticket—and adjust in real time?"

4. The After State
   o   Paint a vivid, emotional future
"Imagine a support team that's proactive, not reactive—solving problems before they escalate."

Anchor the Vision to Their Strategic Goals:
The best Vision Stories tie directly to what buyers care about at the company level: growth, efficiency, risk reduction, or innovation.
This is how you start a demo with direction and end with belief.
Section 4: Building the Workflow Story
Show the story they'll live with—day in, day out.
If the Vision Story inspires belief, the Workflow Story builds trust. This is the heart of your demo—the moment where your buyer sees their daily life transformed. Instead of walking through screens like a tutorial, you walk through them like a story: a day-in-the-life journey with characters, stakes, and success.
This story activates the brain's mirror neurons, helping buyers see themselves using your solution.

Why Workflow Stories Work:
- They reduce abstraction: "I can picture this happening."
- They link features to real human impact
- They demonstrate relevance, not just capability

How to Structure a Workflow Story:

1. Introduce the Character

"Let's say you're Jessica, the intake coordinator."
Instantly grounds the viewer in a relatable role

2. Set the Scene
"It's 8:15 a.m., and she's already behind—20 new tickets, and the routing rules changed overnight."
Creates emotional stakes

3. Present the Challenge
"Normally, she'd spend two hours sorting, prioritizing, and emailing teams."
Highlights the cost of the status quo

4. Demo the Turnaround
"Now watch what happens with our platform—Jessica clicks once, and the entire queue is routed in 15 seconds."
Shows transformation in action

5. End with Resolution
"She's out of firefighting mode and into proactive work by 9:00."
Provides emotional closure and business value

Tip: Use Language of Emotion and Impact
Use phrases like "saves her an hour," "gives her clarity," or "lets her lead"—not just "reduces effort." That language is what makes the story stick.
Up next, we'll discuss how to weave in Detail Stories—without derailing your narrative.

Section 5: Supporting with Detail Stories

Details build credibility—if you control how and when they show up.

The final layer of your Story Stack is the Detail Story. These are the technical, compliance, or process-specific explanations that give your solution depth and legitimacy. But here's the trap: many presenters lead with these stories—overwhelming the audience or derailing the narrative flow. The key is to anchor details to context and only dive in when the moment calls for it.

Why Detail Stories Matter
- They reduce risk perception: "This vendor knows their stuff."
- They satisfy technical buyers and due diligence stages
- They show real-world thinking—not just pitch polish

But unless guided by interest or need, too many details too early will bury your message.

How to Use Detail Stories Effectively
1. Treat Them as "Opt-In" Layers
    o Frame them as optional depth, not core narrative
"I can show you exactly how that's configured—if that's helpful."
Gives the buyer control over how deep you go
2. Use Transitions, Not Tangents
    o Bridge from story to detail clearly
"You just saw the auto-routing in action. Behind the scenes, here's how the logic is managed."

Keeps the flow intact
3. Tailor to Role and Risk
    o Save deep dives for IT, compliance, or legal stakeholders
    o Highlight relevance: "This meets SOC 2 and HIPAA out of the box."
    Makes details feel strategic, not technical trivia

Details Are Trust Builders—Not Story Drivers
Your goal is to fortify the narrative, not fragment it. Think of Detail Stories as evidence exhibits: always available, but revealed with purpose.

Section 6: Delivering a Seamless Stack in Real-Time

The best storytellers don't just know the story—they know when to switch stories.

In a live demo, no matter how well you've prepared your narrative, the audience's attention, questions, and priorities can shift. That's why mastering the real-time delivery of your Story Stack is critical. You need to move smoothly between the vision, workflow, and detail layers—without losing coherence or momentum.
Think of it like jazz: you know the structure, but you can improvise with skill when the room changes tempo.

What Cognitive Science Says
- The brain retains structure better than spontaneity—but engagement thrives on responsiveness
- Stories with clear transitions help the audience follow along even when depth changes
- Layered storytelling supports different learning styles and roles simultaneously

How to Pivot Between Layers Smoothly
1. Use Bridge Phrases
"Let's zoom in for a second on how that's configured behind the scenes..."
"Now stepping back to the big picture—why this matters..."
Helps the audience stay grounded in context

2. Listen for Layer Cues
   - A VP asking "How does this align with OKRs?" →
     Vision Story
   - A user asking "What would this change in my
     workflow?" → Workflow Story
   - An IT lead asking "Is this API-based?" → Detail
     Story
     Aligns your story with the audience's thinking path
3. Close the Loop on Every Pivot
   - Always bring the conversation back to the overall
     value narrative

"That's the detail—and it supports the speed and clarity we talked about at the top."

Train Your Champion to Tell the Stack
The ultimate goal? Equip your internal champion to retell all three layers in their own words. That's how your demo turns into internal momentum.

Chapter 16: Designing for Consensus

One demo. Many minds. One decision.

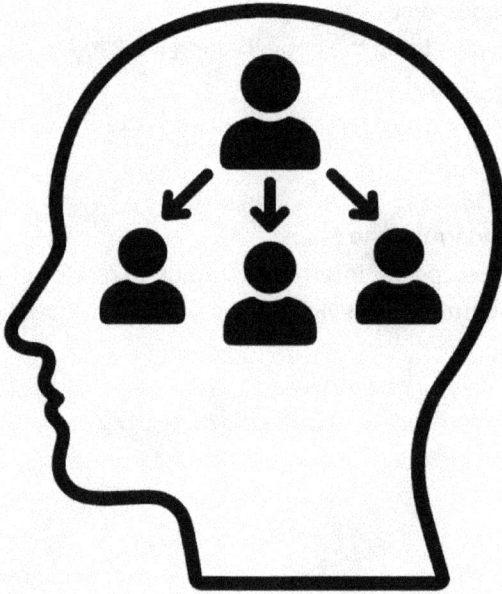

In modern B2B sales, decisions aren't made by one person—
they're made by buying committees. Each stakeholder brings
different goals, roles, and fears to the table. Your demo has to
speak to all of them—not equally, but strategically. This chapter
focuses on designing and delivering demos that account for group
psychology, stakeholder diversity, and internal influence
dynamics.

Section 1: Understanding the Buying Braintrust

*You're not demoing to one person. You're demoing to a
committee—some of whom won't speak until after you're gone.*

In today's B2B landscape, most purchases aren't made by a single
decision-maker. They're made by a group—a "braintrust" of
stakeholders from different functions, each with unique priorities,
fears, and influence. If your demo only resonates with one type of
buyer, it won't get consensus. And without consensus, you won't
get the deal.

That's why your demo must be designed to speak to diverse minds
in the same room—not with generic messaging, but with targeted
story beats that show each stakeholder:

"This solution understands me."

Common Stakeholders in the Demo Room:

    1.   The Executive Sponsor

- o   Focus: Strategic goals, big picture outcomes
- o   Concern: ROI, risk, alignment with company vision

2. The Power User / Champion
    - o   Focus: Workflow improvement, daily pain points
    - o   Concern: Ease of use, relevance, adoption

3. The Technical Evaluator
    - o   Focus: Integrations, scalability, security
    - o   Concern: Feasibility, architecture, long-term support

4. The Skeptic
    - o   Focus: Flaws, red flags, counterpoints
    - o   Concern: Hype vs. reality, cost vs. benefit

5. The Executive Approver / C-Suite
    - o   Focus: Business case, strategic fit
    - o   Concern: Political visibility, future-proofing

Demo Mistake: Treating Them All the Same:

When your narrative assumes a single audience, it alienates others. The key to success is recognizing who's in the room and knowing how to signal value for each—without derailing your story.

In the next section, we'll map these roles to their unique cognitive motives—so you can design content that lands with everyone.

Section 2: Mapping Cognitive Motives by Role

Different minds process the same demo differently.

Every stakeholder in a demo is filtering your message through their role, responsibility, and risk lens. What excites one person may worry another. That's why effective demo design requires role-based cognitive empathy—an understanding of what each person is actually trying to learn, confirm, or defend.

When you tailor your narrative to hit these mental checkboxes, your story resonates across the room—not just with the loudest voice.

What Each Role is Thinking (Even if They Don't Say It)

1. Executive Sponsor
    o "Does this move the needle on our KPIs?"
    o "Can this scale with our goals?"
    o Wants strategic clarity and long-term impact
2. Power User / Champion
    o "Will this make my life easier?"
    o "Can I get my team on board quickly?"
    o Needs emotional and functional relevance
3. Technical Evaluator
    o "Is it secure, stable, and compatible with what we have?"
    o "Can we actually implement and maintain this?"
    o Looks for feasibility and risk reduction

4. Skeptic
    o "What's the catch?"
    o "Where could this break?"
    o Needs transparency and control
5. C-Suite Approver
    o "Does this align with our strategic direction?"
    o "Will I have to defend this decision later?"
    o Demands narrative confidence and minimal friction

Design Your Demo Like a Multi-Channel Story:

Use layered storytelling, targeted examples, and role-specific framing to speak to each mind—often in the same sentence: "This auto-routing saves your ops team hours, reduces error rates for compliance, and frees up leadership visibility."
Next, we'll examine where demos often fracture consensus—and how to avoid losing the room.

Section 3: Fracture Points – Where Demos Lose the Room

You didn't lose the deal—you lost the room. Quietly.

Demos often go sideways not because of what's said, but because of what's missed. When a demo favors one stakeholder's perspective too heavily—or fails to acknowledge another's concerns—fracture points form. These gaps in attention, relevance, or emotional connection don't always show up immediately. But they surface in the debrief, in the group Slack chat, or in the next internal meeting you're not invited to. Knowing how and where demos lose the room gives you the power to keep the group aligned.

Three Common Fracture Points

1. Single-Audience Syndrome
   o The entire demo is geared toward one role (often the champion or decision-maker)
   o Others feel like spectators, not participants

Result: Silence during the demo, resistance after the call

2. Unbalanced Depth
   o Too technical for business leaders
   o Too high-level for evaluators

Result: Confusion, frustration, or mental checkout

3. Unacknowledged Concerns
   o Risk, change management, and user adoption are glossed over
   o No invitation for dissent or discussion

Result: Hidden objections and slow decision cycles

What Fractures Feel Like (in Real Time)

- Sudden camera turn-offs or muted reactions

- Shift in body language: checking out, leaning back
- Lack of follow-up questions from previously engaged stakeholders

How to Prevent Fractures

- Use role-bridging language ("For IT, this runs serverless. For ops, it's hands-off.")
- Check in explicitly ("Would this work for how your team is structured?")
- Invite counterpoints with confidence ("Any concerns this might raise for your side?")

Up next: how to build a multi-role narrative that prevents fractures and fosters alignment.

Section 4: Building a Multi-Role Narrative

One story. Many lenses.

A strong demo doesn't bounce between audiences—it builds a narrative that's rich enough to resonate with all of them at once. That's the art of the multi-role narrative: a layered, role-aware approach that connects the dots across departments without diluting your message.

Instead of trying to please everyone separately, you design story beats that carry relevance for multiple stakeholders simultaneously.

Why Multi-Role Narratives Work

- They streamline delivery and reduce repetition
- They demonstrate fluency in the buyer's organization
- They prevent internal misalignment by creating shared context

Your goal is to create moments where different minds nod at the same time—for different reasons.

How to Build One

1. Use Dual-Benefit Framing

"This dashboard gives leadership a 10,000-foot view—and lets frontline teams drill into day-to-day operations."

Shows how one feature serves two roles

2. Stack Outcomes by Function

"Fewer intake delays for ops. Tighter audit trails for compliance. Better forecasting for finance."

Rapid-fire alignment across departments

3. Sequence Content to Build Collective Momentum
   - Start with vision to engage leadership
   - Move to workflow to engage users
   - Use detail selectively to satisfy skeptics and technical leads
     Mirrors the Story Stack structure across stakeholders

4. Visually Represent Role Impact

- o Color-code personas in slides or show their
  workflows side-by-side

  Helps everyone "see themselves" in the story

Make Every Stakeholder Feel Seen

When people feel their needs were addressed—and others' were too—they leave aligned, not fragmented.

Next, we'll explore how to empower your internal champion to carry that alignment forward.

Section 5: Empowering the Internal Champion

The most important part of your demo happens after you leave.

No matter how polished your presentation is, the deal often hinges on someone else's ability to retell your story when you're not there. That someone is your internal champion—the person who believes in your solution and is willing to fight for it internally. But even great champions need help. Without the right tools and language, their advocacy can get diluted, misquoted, or lost in translation.

Your job isn't just to impress them. It's to equip them.

Why Champions Struggle to Retell Your Story

- They're not demo pros—they're busy, overtasked insiders
- They might lack technical fluency or persuasive confidence

- They forget nuanced details, or oversimplify your value prop

This creates a cognitive breakdown: your story degrades as it spreads.

How to Equip Champions for Internal Retelling:

1. Provide a Role-Specific Recap

Send a brief summary that speaks to each stakeholder group's takeaway

Gives your champion quick reference points to share

2. Create a One-Slide "Demo Memory"

   o Visual summary of pain → solution → impact

   Helps buyers pitch your product internally with confidence

3. Supply Framing Language

"You can describe it like this: 'It's like a control tower for intake— gives us visibility, saves time, and adapts fast.'"

Turns your insight into their internal soundbite

4. Make Next Steps Easy to Champion

   o Share pilot options, timelines, or sample workflows

   Reduces the mental load required to push forward

Your Story Wins When They Can Repeat It:

The mark of a great demo isn't what happens on the call—it's what happens after. Empower your champion, and you multiply your message.

Chapter 17: Mastering the Pivot

You can't control every moment—but you can control how you respond to it

No matter how tightly you prepare your presentation, buyers will interrupt, shift direction, or throw curveballs mid-demo. The best demo professionals don't panic or bulldoze forward—they pivot with purpose. This chapter teaches how to recognize and execute cognitive pivots that keep engagement intact and decision momentum high.

Section 1: The Psychology of Unexpected Shifts

Even the best-planned demos go off-script. The best presenters know what to do when they do.

In a live software demo, things rarely go exactly as planned. Stakeholders arrive late. Questions arise out of order. A feature fails. Or the executive who was checked out suddenly asks a hard-hitting question.

What happens next separates average demo delivery from exceptional demo agility.

From a cognitive perspective, unexpected shifts trigger a stress response—for you *and* your audience. The human brain favors predictability and narrative flow. When those get disrupted, our working memory can become flooded, attention may splinter, and trust can erode if the presenter seems unsure.

But here's the good news: how you handle the pivot is often more memorable than the pivot itself.

Your Brain on a Demo Disruption:

When a demo derails, your brain:

- Shifts from executive function (planned delivery) into reactive mode

- May enter a fight/flight/freeze response—even subtly

- Experiences a drop in verbal fluidity, tone modulation, and recall precision

In these moments, you must lean on training, not instinct.

Your Audience's Brain on a Pivot:

- They notice your body language and vocal tone instantly

- If you seem flustered, they infer the product might be fragile too

- If you pivot with confidence, they perceive flexibility and competence

The Pivot Principle:

A great pivot isn't a detour—it's a recommitment to relevance.

Next, we'll learn to recognize the subtle signals that tell you when to pivot, and how to do it *before* you lose the room.

Section 2: Recognizing Pivot Cues in Real Time

The audience will always tell you what they need—if you're paying attention.

A well-timed pivot isn't random—it's a response to a signal. These signals can be verbal, nonverbal, or contextual. The most effective demo professionals aren't just presenting—they're listening and watching for the subtle shifts that indicate it's time to change course.

If you wait for disengagement to become obvious, you've already lost momentum. The key is recognizing pivot cues early—and adjusting your narrative while keeping control.

Verbal Pivot Cues:

- "Actually, what we're more curious about is..."
- "Can you show us how this would work for the intake team?"
- "That's good, but what about security compliance?"
- These aren't interruptions—they're invitations to reframe your value

Nonverbal Pivot Cues:

- Leaning back, checking phones, turning off cameras
- Sudden silence or drop in note-taking
- Side-channel activity (e.g., chatting in Zoom or Slack)
- Indicates disengagement or confusion—time to shift gears

Contextual Pivot Cues:

- New stakeholder joins mid-demo
- Unexpected technical delay or glitch
- A slide or screen sparks more excitement than planned
- Requires spontaneous reordering or deepening of content

Read the Room, Re-route the Flow:

Great demos are dynamic. If you're rigid, the buyer sees inflexibility—not just in you, but in your product.

Train yourself to treat these cues as opportunities, not detours.

Next, we'll explore the three types of cognitive pivots you can execute mid-demo—each with a different function and impact.

Section 3: The Three Types of Effective Pivots

Not every shift is the same. Learn which kind of pivot the moment demands.

When a live demo veers off course—or more accurately, evolves in real time—you have more than one way to adjust. Think of pivoting not as a single maneuver, but as a toolbox of directional shifts, each designed to keep attention, relevance, and trust intact.

Here are the three most effective pivot types in high-stakes software demos:

1. Content Pivot – Changing What You're Showing

When to use:

- The audience shows more interest in a different module or use case

- A stakeholder asks for a specific scenario earlier than planned

How it works:

- Acknowledge the shift ("Let's jump ahead to what that looks like…")

- Reframe the flow to match their immediate curiosity
- Always close the loop and return to your core arc

2. Role Pivot – Changing Who You're Speaking To

When to use:

- A quiet stakeholder suddenly asks a role-specific question
- You realize a key decision-maker is not being addressed

How it works:

- Shift your language and example set
- Pull that role's value lens into focus

"From IT's perspective, here's what's happening under the hood..."

3. ☐ Tone Pivot – Changing How You're Presenting

When to use:

- Energy is dropping, or engagement feels flat
- A tense or skeptical question surfaces

How it works:

- Adjust pace, tone, or formality
- Use humor, stories, or directness to re-engage

"That's a fair question. Let's walk through that together."

Each of these pivots keeps your narrative alive—without surrendering your structure.

Next: we'll explore cognitive techniques to make these pivots seamless and natural in the moment.

Section 4: Cognitive Techniques for Smooth Pivots

When you pivot, the story shouldn't feel broken—it should feel upgraded.

The difference between a smooth pivot and a jarring one lies in cognitive continuity. Your audience is building a mental map of the demo as it unfolds. If you pivot too abruptly—without signaling or context—you disrupt that map. But if you pivot intentionally, using the right language and structure, you enhance credibility and keep attention intact.

Here are the most effective techniques to pivot without breaking the narrative flow:

1. Use Bridge Language

Transitions help the audience follow your logic:

- "Let's zoom in on that workflow for a second."

- "Before we go deeper, let me show how this looks from IT's perspective."

- "That's a great question—let's anchor that to what we just saw."

Signals a controlled, relevant detour—not a derailment.

2. Reset Context

After the pivot, re-orient the audience by restating your structure:

"We just looked at how this streamlines intake. Now let's connect that to your audit concerns."

Prevents disorientation and reinforces narrative clarity.

3. Echo the Original Goal

Remind the group why the pivot still serves the original intent:

"This ties directly back to reducing ticket volume—just from the IT angle."

Reinforces value and keeps everyone aligned.

4. Narrate with Confidence

Don't apologize for the shift. Frame it as responsiveness:

"Let's adapt—this sounds like where your team's focus really is."

Buyers appreciate flexibility when it's delivered with poise.

Smooth pivots show that you're not just presenting—you're thinking in real time. Next, we'll discuss how to train for this agility before stepping into high-stakes demos.

Section 5: Training for Agility

You won't rise to the level of your demo script—you'll fall to the level of your preparation.

Great pivoting looks effortless. But behind that ease is deliberate practice. You don't become agile in the moment—you become agile in rehearsal. The most confident demo professionals prepare for disruption the way pilots train for turbulence: by simulating it until adaptive response becomes second nature.

This section gives you practical techniques to build the cognitive reflexes you'll need when the stakes are high and the plan goes sideways.

1. Rehearse Demo Disruptions

Set up mock demos with a colleague or coach and introduce surprise variables:

- Stakeholder joins late

- Someone questions ROI or feasibility midstream

- A feature doesn't work as planned

Practice recovering while staying composed and clear

2. Map Common Pivot Scenarios

Build a list of predictable pivot points based on your audience types:

- Executive asks for outcomes earlier

- IT wants to go deeper on architecture

- End user is confused by workflow language

Prepare mini-narratives for each so they're ready on demand

3. Build a Demo Pivot Toolkit

Create a mental or visual toolkit with:

- Bridge phrases for smooth transitions

- Visual slides or dashboards you can jump to quickly

- One-slide pivots that re-center the value proposition

Gives you options without abandoning structure

4. Train Emotional Control

Practice intentional breathing, voice modulation, and pacing under pressure.

Keeps you grounded, even when your internal state spikes

The best demo performers don't just know their content—they're ready to shift without skipping a beat.

Chapter 18: The Neuroscience of Objections

Objections aren't obstacles—they're cognitive signals.

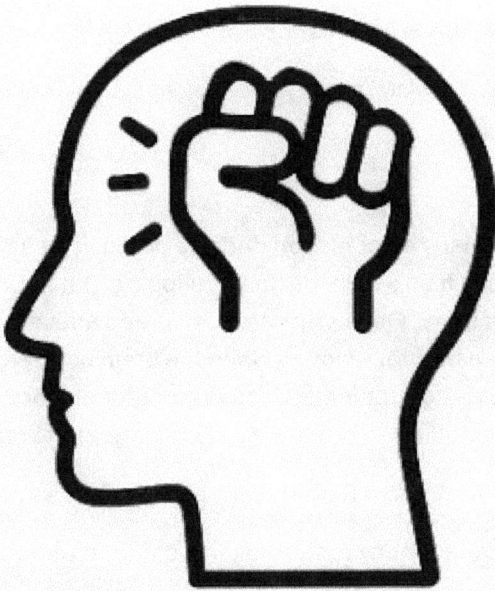

Objections in a software demo are often misunderstood. Many presenters see them as friction or failure. In reality, objections are a sign of engagement—an indicator that the brain is actively testing, challenging, and processing your message. This chapter explores the neuroscience behind resistance, how to decode it, and how to respond in ways that preserve momentum and build trust.

Section 1: Why the Brain Pushes Back

Objections aren't resistance to you—they're resistance to uncertainty.

When a buyer raises an objection during a demo, it's easy to take it personally or see it as a sign the deal is slipping. But neuroscience tells a different story. Objections are actually cognitive defense mechanisms—a natural reaction when the brain perceives a threat, a gap, or a contradiction. In that moment, the brain isn't rejecting your solution—it's doing its job to protect the status quo.

The Brain's Priority: Avoid Regret, Risk, and Embarrassment

The brain's default setting is survival. In a demo, that translates to:

- Avoiding decisions that could lead to blame
- Rejecting information that feels too unfamiliar or misaligned
- Defending current mental models to reduce mental effort

When someone objects, they're signaling:

"You've activated a part of my brain that needs resolution—not a rebuttal."

Objection ≠ Disinterest

In fact, many objections signal the opposite:

- "How does this integrate with our system?" = *I'm picturing us using it*

- "That seems like a lot of change." = *I'm evaluating impact*

- "We've tried tools like this before." = *I'm comparing and protecting*

Your job is not to defeat the objection—it's to decode what the brain is really saying.

Demo Mindset Shift:

Stop fearing objections. Start treating them as feedback loops—cognitive check-ins that reveal what the buyer's brain needs in order to move forward.

Next, we'll break down the four cognitive roots of objections, so you can diagnose resistance in real time and respond strategically.

Section 2: The Four Cognitive Roots of Objections

Every objection has a mental trigger. Understand the root, and you'll know how to respond.

Not all objections are created equal. Some stem from confusion. Others, from fear. Still others, from pride, pressure, or past experience. If you treat every objection the same, you risk overexplaining, under-listening, or addressing the wrong issue altogether.

This section breaks down the four core cognitive roots of objections—what triggers them, how they sound, and how to reframe them in real time.

1. Cognitive Dissonance

"This doesn't match what I know, believe, or expect."

Examples:

- "We don't do things that way."

- "That's not how our team is structured."
  What it means:

- You've introduced a concept that conflicts with their mental model
  What to do:

- Realign with shared values or reference peer examples

- Reframe the concept as evolution, not contradiction

2. Cognitive Overload

"This is too much information, too fast."

Examples:

- "I'm not following this part."

- "Wait—can you go back?"
  What it means:

- Working memory is overwhelmed
  What to do:

- Slow down, chunk content, and visually anchor key takeaways

3. Cognitive Risk

"If I back this, will I get blamed if it fails?"

Examples:

- "What's your track record in our industry?"

- "How hard is this to implement?"
  What it means:

- They're assessing reputational or operational danger
  What to do:

- Offer proof points, customer examples, and de-risking options

4. Cognitive Bias

"I already believe something that conflicts with this."

Examples:

- "We've tried tools like this—it didn't work."

- "I don't like subscription models."
  What it means:

- A past experience or belief is shaping their judgment
  What to do:

- Validate their experience, then gently reframe with new context

Next, we'll explore how to reframe objections without increasing resistance or sounding defensive.

Section 3: Reframing vs. Resisting

Argue with the brain, and you'll lose. Align with it, and you move forward.

When someone raises an objection in a demo, our instinct is often to defend the product, the process, or ourselves. But from a cognitive standpoint, resistance fuels resistance. If you counter too quickly, the brain perceives threat—and doubles down on its original stance.

The goal isn't to win the point, but to lower the brain's threat level. You don't push back—you pull them forward through reframing.

What Happens When You Push:

When you resist an objection:

- The buyer's brain activates confirmation bias
- They look for new reasons to doubt you
- Emotional tension increases, and trust erodes

Reframing: A Smarter Response:

Reframing means acknowledging the concern, then gently shifting the lens:

"That's a fair concern. And you're right—many teams have felt that way at first. What we've seen is that with the right rollout, adoption actually accelerates because users finally feel in control."

It validates, aligns, and opens a new narrative path.

The Three-Part Reframing Formula:

1. Acknowledge

"Great question—you're not the first to ask that."

2. Align

"We've seen others in your space face similar hesitation."

3. Expand

"What changed the game for them was how easily they were able to train and adapt—especially after week one."

This reduces threat, builds social proof, and shows growth is possible.

The bottom line is that objections aren't battles—they're bridges. Learn to cross them gracefully, and you'll move the buyer forward without friction.

Next, we'll explore tactical techniques for responding to objections live—using story, tone, and structure.

Section 4: Tactical Techniques for Live Objection Handling

The best response isn't always an answer—it's a moment of clarity.

Handling objections in real time requires more than knowledge—it requires control of tone, timing, and structure. A rushed or defensive response can erode trust. A well-paced, empathic reply can reinforce credibility, calm the room, and even turn skeptics into supporters.

This section offers specific techniques to guide your responses when objections surface during a live demo—without derailing momentum or sounding rehearsed.

1. Mirror and Rephrase

"So if I heard you right, your concern is about implementation time—specifically how fast your team could adopt this?"

This shows you're listening and clarifies the true nature of the objection. It also gives the stakeholder a chance to correct or refine their concern before you respond.

2. Bridge and Expand

"Absolutely—implementation timelines are top of mind for many of our clients. What's worked well for teams like yours is a phased rollout that gets early wins fast."Bridges the objection to a positive outcome. Avoids denial. Builds momentum.

3. Story-Based Deflection

"That reminds me of a client who had the exact same hesitation. They were skeptical about adoption too—until they saw how quickly their users took to the new workflow."

Uses narrative to shift the focus and create emotional resonance. Also triggers cognitive empathy and relatability.

4. Recenter on Value

After resolving, quickly bring the conversation back to the value narrative:

"And that's all in service of getting claims processed 40% faster—which is what we're ultimately solving for."

Recentering on value keeps the buyer's brain focused on the bigger picture.

Next, we'll explore how to pre-wire your demo to anticipate and neutralize objections before they surface.

Section 5: Pre-Wiring the Brain to Expect Objections

The best objection handling happens before the objection is raised.

While it's important to respond to objections in real time, elite demo professionals go one step further: they design their presentations to anticipate resistance and reduce it before it ever surfaces. This approach, called pre-wiring, leverages the brain's preference for narrative coherence and emotional safety by gently introducing potential friction points as expected and manageable.

When done well, pre-wiring makes objections feel less risky to raise—and less urgent to dwell on.

Why Pre-Wiring Works:

The brain prefers predictable discomfort over unexpected conflict. By naming a challenge before the buyer does, you lower their cognitive guard.

"You might be wondering how this works with your legacy system—that's something we hear often."

This reframes objections as shared, solvable concerns—not threats.

Tactics to Pre-Wire Your Demo

1. Normalize the Concern

"Many teams we work with were initially unsure about X..."

2. De-Risk the Decision

"That's why we offer both a pilot phase and live support during rollout."

3. Introduce Friction as a Strength

"Yes, this changes your workflow—but that's also what drives the 40% efficiency gain."

4. Use Proof Before the Pushback

"You'll see in this case study that compliance was a big concern— until their auditors saw the traceability features."

Cognitive Outcome:

Pre-wiring helps buyers feel:

- Heard (even before speaking)

- Understood

- Confident that challenges are already solved

This builds trust and smooths the path to consensus.

Chapter 19: The Closing Moment

They won't remember everything. Make sure they remember the right thing.

The end of your demo is more than a wrap-up—it's a neural bookmark. It's the last opportunity to cement your message, clarify value, and prime action. From a cognitive science perspective, people remember the final moment disproportionately well—a phenomenon known as the "recency effect." This chapter teaches you how to close a demo in a way that maximizes retention, creates emotional momentum, and invites forward movement.

Section 1: The Psychology of the Last Impression

What they remember is shaped by how you end.

Demos don't fade out—they leave an imprint. That imprint is shaped more by how you end than by how you begin. In cognitive science, this is called the Recency Effect—the principle that the brain gives disproportionate weight to the final piece of information in a sequence.

In a software demo, this means your close isn't just a formality—it's a memory anchor. It determines how your message will be recalled, re-shared, and acted upon when you're no longer in the room.

Why Recency Matters:

The brain prioritizes information that:

- Comes at the end of an experience
- Is delivered with emotional weight
- Feels personally relevant or high-stakes

That final moment is when short-term memory begins deciding what to store, what to discard, and how to frame what just happened. If your close is vague, rushed, or overly technical, you lose the opportunity to shape perception.

The Cost of a Weak Close

Many demo professionals end with:

- "So yeah... any questions?"

- "That's everything I had to show today."

- A quick summary that sounds more like a sigh than a statement

These endings don't reinforce your message—they dilute it. They leave buyers to piece together what mattered most—and most won't.

The Close as a Neural Bookmark:

A great closing moment doesn't just summarize—it stamps the message with clarity and confidence.

"If you remember just one thing from today: This solution helps you control the chaos, accelerate decisions, and finally get ahead of the volume."

That's what sticks. Next, we'll break down the three goals of a brain-smart close that reinforces memory and motivates movement.

Section 2: The Three Goals of a Cognitive Close

Every closing moment should leave them knowing, feeling, and wanting something.

Closing a demo isn't about ending—it's about activating. A strong close doesn't just summarize features; it cements understanding, fuels motivation, and plants a clear next step in the buyer's mind. If your audience walks away unsure of what mattered or what happens next, you haven't closed—you've coasted.

To avoid that, aim to fulfill these three psychological goals in your final moments:

1. Seal the Value

Reinforce your core message in a way that's simple, emotional, and human:

"You want clarity, speed, and control. That's what this gives you."

This ties the solution back to the original pain and outcome. The buyer's brain needs coherence—a resolution to the problem you opened with.

What to include:

- Restatement of the pain

- Brief reframe of your solution

- A meaningful phrase or metaphor to lock it in

2. Motivate Action

The close should make the path forward feel clear and desirable—not like homework:

"Here are two easy ways to explore this further: a test drive, or a sandbox trial with your real data."

This reduces decision friction and makes action feel accessible.

What to include:

- 1–2 concrete next steps

- Language of invitation, not pressure

- Timeline or urgency only if it adds clarity

3. Anchor Memory

Give them something that sticks:

- A standout phrase: "From chaos to control."

- A visual: before/after dashboard

- A stat: "Teams reduce intake errors by 46%"

Think: *What will they quote later in a meeting?*

Next, we'll walk through how to structure your closing moments to hit these targets seamlessly.

Section 3: Structuring a Brain-Smart Closing Sequence

It's not just what you say—it's how you land it.

A strong demo close isn't improvised. It's intentionally built, just like your opening. And it follows a simple principle: the human brain craves closure. Not just an end—but a moment that feels complete, resolved, and valuable.

Here's a step-by-step structure for crafting a closing sequence that leaves your message echoing long after the meeting ends.

1. Use the Callback Technique

Start your close by tying the end to the beginning. Remind them why they came and show how you delivered:

"When we started, you mentioned the chaos of juggling six intake systems. What you just saw was a unified process—built to simplify that."

Creates narrative symmetry and emotional payoff

2. Deliver a Value Recap in Three Layers

Reinforce the core benefits across three dimensions:

- Emotional: "Less stress, more control."

- Operational: "Fewer intake delays, faster decisions."

- Strategic: "Better visibility, stronger forecasting."

Hits the brain's motivational centers from different angles

3. Prime the Next Step—Softly, Clearly

Don't ask for commitment—offer a clear, low-friction path:

"If you'd like, we can set up a 2-week sandbox so your team can explore it hands-on."

Removes ambiguity without adding pressure

4. Loop in a Cognitive Anchor

End with something that's easy to repeat:

- A metaphor: "It's like a control tower for your workflows."

- A stat: "Teams typically cut intake time by 30% in the first month."

- A phrase: "From friction to flow."

Gives your champion something sticky to share internally

Next, we'll fine-tune the tone and delivery techniques that elevate your closing moments from good to unforgettable.

Section 4: Tone, Pace, and Delivery in the Final Minute

How you sound shapes what they remember.

When it comes to memory, delivery is destiny. You could say all the right words in your close, but if you say them too quickly, too flatly, or with too little conviction, they'll land with a whisper—not a mark.

That final minute is a performance. It's the moment your message transitions from *spoken* to *stored*. The brain doesn't just listen to words—it listens to how you say them. Tone, rhythm, and even silence create the cognitive container that locks your message in.

1. Slow Down—Deliberately

The brain needs time to encode meaning. When you slow your speech during the final minute:

- You signal importance

- You create emotional space

- You sound more intentional and confident

"What this means... is fewer delays... more decisions made... and less fire-fighting."

Let each phrase breathe

2. Use Tone to Add Weight

- Lower your vocal register slightly to sound grounded

- Use emphasis sparingly—reserve it for critical words

- Avoid filler words or trailing off at sentence ends

Confidence, not volume, makes people lean in

3. Embrace the Pause

Silence isn't awkward—it's powerful. A 1–2 second pause after your final value statement gives the brain space to absorb.

"...And that's why teams call this their decision engine." *[pause]*

Pauses create gravity. They make your audience reflect, not just hear.

Avoid the "Fade-Out Close"

No: "Okay, so... yeah, that's it unless you have questions."
Yes: "Let's talk next steps when you're ready—but more than anything, thanks for your time and attention today."

Next, we'll explore leave-behind tools and memory anchors that extend your demo's impact beyond the moment.

Section 5: Post-Close Echo Tools

The demo ends—but your message keeps going.

Even a great close fades with time. That's why the best demo professionals don't stop at the final screen—they leave behind echoes. These are the cognitive reinforcements that help your message stick, spread, and resurface long after the call ends.

Whether your champion is presenting to others, reflecting on what they saw, or just sorting through multiple vendors, these post-demo tools ensure your narrative stays top of mind.

1. The Leave-Behind Summary

Provide a clean, simple recap that matches the flow of your demo—not just a feature list.

- One-pager with value bullets and key visuals
- Highlights pain points, outcomes, and next steps
- Designed for quick internal sharing

Makes your champion look smart while keeping your message intact

2. Use Metaphors to Anchor Memory

"Think of it like mission control for your intake process."
"It's your claims co-pilot—smart, fast, and always watching."

Metaphors convert abstract ideas into mental images, which the brain retains more easily than raw text.

Gives your message a shape buyers can visualize and repeat

3. Highlight One Sticky Metric

Pick a single, meaningful result—then make it easy to remember:

"Teams saw a 42% drop in intake cycle time within the first 60 days."

Numbers give your narrative credibility and urgency

4. Equip Your Champion with Talking Points

Send a follow-up that includes:

- Recap of goals and demo highlights

- Suggested responses to likely objections

- Callbacks to internal priorities or pain points mentioned

Turns your buyer into your internal storyteller

With these echo tools, your demo doesn't end at goodbye—it keeps selling in the rooms you're not in.

Chapter 20: The Post-Demo Follow-Up

Your demo doesn't end when the screen goes dark. That's when the decision-making begins.

The most important decisions about your product often happen after the demo. Yet most follow-up emails are generic, overly polite, or focused on scheduling. This chapter reframes post-demo communication as a neuroscience-driven extension of the presentation—a strategic moment to reinforce memory, clarify value, and rebuild mental engagement.

Buyers forget fast. Your job is to remind them what mattered, why it matters, and what to do next.

Section 1: The Science of Forgetting

The brain isn't built to remember everything—it's built to filter.

As powerful as your demo may have felt in the moment, the buyer's brain has already started to forget it. Cognitive science tells us that memory is designed to decay unless it's reinforced. In fact, most people forget up to 80% of new information within 48 hours— especially when it's complex, technical, or emotionally neutral.

That means your most compelling insights, your smoothest transitions, even your clever analogies, all begin to fade the moment the call ends.

The Forgetting Curve:

Developed by psychologist Hermann Ebbinghaus, the forgetting curve shows that memory drops steeply after learning unless actively retained. The brain:

- Prioritizes emotionally resonant, personally relevant content

- Discards neutral, complex, or competing information
- Needs repetition, retrieval, and spacing to build long-term memory

Why This Matters for Demos:

Your audience:

- May leave your demo impressed—but can't rearticulate what they saw
- Might struggle to explain the solution to internal stakeholders
- Is likely seeing multiple demos in the same week

Without reinforcement, even a great demo fades into a blur.

The Strategic Opportunity

Post-demo communication isn't a formality—it's a neurological intervention. It's your chance to:

- Reactivate the brain's memory pathways
- Re-establish emotional engagement
- Make your message sticky enough to survive the internal gauntlet

Forget the generic "Thanks for your time" email. What your buyer's brain needs is a reminder that feels like a revival.

Next, we'll look at the three cognitive jobs your follow-up must perform to be remembered and acted on.

Section 2: The Three Cognitive Jobs of Post-Demo Follow-Up

You're not just sending an email—you're rebuilding the mental map.

Once the demo ends, your buyer's brain begins reorganizing. It files, compresses, and forgets. But it also leaves placeholders— "this seemed important, but I'll revisit later." Your follow-up must do more than thank them for their time. It must reactivate the right neural pathways and rebuild the cognitive scaffolding for your value proposition.

To do this well, your post-demo communication needs to do three distinct jobs:

1. Recall: Help Them Remember What They Saw

Your buyer likely attended multiple demos—or had four other meetings that day. Without a clear memory refresh, your message fades.

"Here's a quick recap of what we covered: reducing intake volume, improving visibility, and streamlining compliance—all in one workflow."

Use short, high-impact summaries that echo demo phrasing and structure.

2. Relevance: Make It About Them Again

Tie the demo explicitly back to their pain points and goals— personalized, not generic.

"You mentioned your team's struggling with case delays. What we showed was designed to give them real-time alerts before bottlenecks build."

Reinforces that you were listening—and that the demo wasn't canned.

3. Roadmap: Show What's Next—Without Pressure

Ambiguity kills momentum. A follow-up should create clarity without feeling aggressive.

"There are two easy ways forward from here:

1. Set up a sandbox with your data

2. Or join a 30-min Q&A with our solutions engineer"

Give clear next steps, framed as options, not obligations.

When your follow-up does these three jobs—recall, relevance, and roadmap—you're not just following up. You're extending the demo's impact inside their mind.

Section 3: Writing Brain-Smart Follow-Up Emails

If they only read one thing after the demo, make it count.

Most post-demo emails follow the same formula: a thank-you, a vague recap, and a hopeful nudge to schedule next steps. But if you want your message to stick, spread, and spark action, your email must be more than polite—it must be designed for cognitive reactivation.

This section outlines the elements of a brain-smart follow-up—one that refreshes memory, rebuilds motivation, and makes next steps easy.

1. Lead with a Cognitive Hook

Start with a bold reminder of value—not a soft thank-you:

"Yesterday you saw how teams are cutting intake delays by 42% with a single workflow."

Activates memory with a stat, metaphor, or result—not just courtesy.

2. Echo the Story, Not Just the Software

Recap the demo in narrative form:

- Reference their pain points
- Tie back to the core journey (problem → process → payoff)
- Use simple, conversational language

"You shared that your team is overwhelmed by duplicate claims. What we showed was how auto-prioritization clears the noise so nothing slips through."

This type of phrasing reinforces emotional relevance and comprehension.

3. Include One Visual or Diagram

The brain loves images, especially ones it saw in the demo. Reuse a key screenshot, summary visual, or comparison chart. Visuals activate recognition faster than text alone.

4. Offer a Next Step—Without Pressure

"Would it help to explore a test environment? Or would you prefer a quick Q&A to align internally first?"

Offering choices gives control and encourages action.

Brain-smart follow-ups feel personal, confident, and actionable. They don't just nudge—they guide.

Section 4: Timing and Spacing Strategies

The right message at the wrong time is forgotten.

Even the most thoughtful follow-up won't stick if it's mis-timed. That's because memory isn't just about what you say, it's about when you say it. Cognitive psychology shows that spacing your messages over time strengthens retention. This is known as spaced repetition, and it's one of the most powerful tools in post-demo communication.

This section outlines how to use timing and spacing to reinforce memory without annoying your buyer.

1. The 1–1–3 Cadence

Send follow-ups on this schedule:

- 1 hour after the demo: Quick recap email with value summary and next step options
- 1 day later: A short piece of reinforcement content (video clip, case study, or key visual)
- 3 days later: A gentle check-in or additional resource aligned to their specific role or concern

Mirrors how the brain encodes and strengthens memory pathways.

2. Micro-Content for Re-Engagement

Buyers don't need long documents—they need small, meaningful nudges:

- A 60-second screen recording of a key feature

- A 1-page PDF titled "What We Heard. What We Showed."

- A visual use-case map with their priorities circled

Keeps you present without adding cognitive load.

3. Wait and Watch—Don't Over-Chase

If a buyer pauses communication, allow space for internal processing. Look for:

- Opens and clicks in your recap email

- Forwarding behavior

- Replays of shared demo videos

Signals cognitive reactivation—respond with value, not pressure.

Right pacing respects attention and amplifies memory. You're not reminding them you exist—you're helping them rebuild the case in their mind.

Next, we'll explore how to support your internal champion so they can carry your message forward with clarity and confidence.

Section 5: How to Support the Internal Champion Post-Demo

You're no longer the presenter—they are.

After the demo ends, the buying process goes behind closed doors. Your success now depends on someone else telling your story—usually your internal champion. But here's the problem: they weren't trained to demo your product. They're not wired to recall your phrasing, your framing, or your metaphors. Without support, your message gets diluted, misunderstood, or lost entirely.

This is where smart demo professionals shine. They don't just demo, but they equip champions to carry the torch.

1. Give Them a Demo Memory Kit

Send a post-demo package designed for easy internal sharing:

- A clean one-pager: problem, process, payoff

- A short explainer video or clip from the demo

- A few talking points tied to their pain points

Makes them look prepared and persuasive without extra work

2. Anticipate Internal Objections

Equip your champion with light rebuttals to likely concerns:

- "It looks complicated" → "Actually, we saw how the workflows mirror what we already do"

- "Is this secure enough?" → "They're HIPAA and SOC 2 compliant out of the box"

Reduces the chance your message is undercut in your absence

3. Follow Up With Role-Specific Content

If they have to brief finance, ops, or IT:

- Send targeted slides or brief assets for each

- Use relevant terms, priorities, and success metrics

The follow-up content helps your message cross internal silos with consistency. When you support your champion cognitively, they become an extension of your demo. Their success is your success.

Chapter 21: Measuring Demo Effectiveness

What gets measured gets remembered, and improved.

Cognitive science doesn't just inform how we design demos—it also gives us new ways to measure their impact. Traditional demo metrics (like meeting length or number of features shown) tell us little about how the buyer's brain responded. This chapter reframes demo measurement as a feedback loop, where memory, engagement, and behavior guide how you evolve and sharpen your delivery.

Section 1: Rethinking Demo Success Metrics

What if your demo felt great, but nothing stuck?

Too often, sales teams evaluate demos by how they felt: Was the audience engaged? Did the tech work? Were there good vibes in the room? But feelings are not outcomes. From a cognitive perspective, a successful demo does not go smoothly; it's remembered, retold, and acted upon.

To truly measure demo effectiveness, we need to move beyond activity-based metrics and focus on cognitive impact. Typical metrics tracked with presentations include:

- Time spent presenting
- Number of features shown
- Number of attendees
- Volume of slides

The issue with the typical metrics is that they don't tell you what truly matters. They reflect completion, not comprehension. A 45-minute demo that leaves the buyer confused is not better than a 15-minute session that lands a clear, memorable message.

What Cognitive Metrics Ask Instead:

- Was the value clearly understood?

- Could the buyer re-explain it to others after the call?

- Did the story stick enough to spark internal momentum?

These are perception-based outcomes, and while harder to quantify, they're essential to success in modern, consensus-driven buying environments.

The Mindset Shift:

Start treating your demo as a learning experience, not just a sales interaction. You're not just transferring information; you're triggering new understanding.

So ask:

"What did this demo change in the buyer's mind?"

Until you answer that, you haven't measured what matters.

Up next: we'll explore the real-time cognitive cues, both the verbal and nonverbal, that signal how well your demo is landing in the moment.

Section 2: Cognitive Signals to Watch During the Demo

Engagement is visible—if you know where to look.

Buyers don't usually say, "I'm confused," or "This is amazing!" But their minds speak subtle signals, verbal, nonverbal, and behavioral cues that reveal how well your demo is landing in real time. Recognizing these signals allows you to adjust on the fly, reinforce critical moments, or pause to reframe when needed.

This section helps you identify and interpret those cues through a cognitive lens.

Verbal Cues: Signals of Friction or Flow

- Clarification requests

"Can you go back to that part again?"

May signal overload, dissonance, or missed context

- Future-focused questions

"How would this integrate with our systems?"

Indicates interest and cognitive projection—engagement is high

- Paraphrasing or reframing

"So you're saying we could cut our approval time in half?"

Confirms understanding and emotional resonance

Virtual and Nonverbal Cues:

In person:

- Leaning in, focused gaze = high attention
- Crossed arms, diverted eyes = disconnection or skepticism

On a virtual meeting:

- Camera on with steady eye contact = active focus

- Frequent glancing away, typing = distraction or disengagement

Use these cues to know when to pause, summarize, or ask a quick question to re-engage.

Behavioral Signals:

- Taking notes or screenshots

- Bookmarking a part of the screen share

- Asking for a copy of a chart or workflow

These are "cognitive bookmarks"—moments the brain deems worth remembering

When you train yourself to spot these real-time cues, you no longer guess if your demo is working—you see it happening.

Section 3: Post-Demo Signals That Matter

What happens after the demo reveals what truly landed.

Your demo may be over, but the real test is what happens after. The brain processes new information in layers—often outside your view. While you can't sit inside the buyer's mind, you can observe behavioral traces that reveal how well your message survived the memory filter.

In this section, we decode the post-demo signals that matter most—not just as sales indicators, but as cognitive validation.

1. Engagement with Your Follow-Up

- Do they open your email within the first few hours?

- Do they click on links or download attached resources?

- Was the email forwarded internally?

These actions show active retrieval—the buyer's brain is trying to reinforce and share the value you presented.

2. Quality of Questions in Follow-Up Conversations

- Shallow questions = retained facts

- Strategic, "what-if" questions = retained meaning

"Could this scale across our three regional teams?" → Indicates the buyer understood the core concept and is applying it to their world.

This is a sign that the value story has moved from passive listening to internal modeling.

3. Re-Engagement Requests

- "Can you show this to our VP of Ops?"

- "We want to see that reporting dashboard again."

- "Can we do a deeper dive with our IT lead?"

These are cognitive markers of internal storytelling—your champion is repeating your demo to others, which means your message was clear, memorable, and persuasive.

Not all post-demo activity means progress—but the right patterns show that your message is still alive, still moving, and still working on their brain.

Section 4: Creating a Demo Scorecard Based on Cognitive Response

Forget "Did it go well?" Ask: "What did their brain retain?"

Most demo reviews focus on performance: Did I say the right things? Did I hit the feature list? Did they smile? But to truly improve demo impact, you need to assess it through a cognitive lens—what was remembered, what was misunderstood, and what was compelling enough to repeat.

This section offers a practical framework to build your own Cognitive Demo Scorecard—so you can track not just delivery, but mental resonance.

1. Emotional Resonance

Did they show signs of connecting emotionally with the value?

- Repeated your key phrases?

- Nodded during transformation stories?

- Reacted positively to your metaphor or stat?

Score: 1–5
Indicates alignment with the problem narrative and emotional urgency

2. Conceptual Clarity

Did they understand the "why," not just the "what"?

- Asked strategic questions, not just technical ones

- Could rephrase your solution in their own words

- Expressed recognition: "This is exactly what we need."

Score: 1–5
✓ Reflects message clarity and simplicity

3. Transferable Narrative

Can your champion retell your story internally?

- Requested leave-behinds or decks

- Shared your phrasing in a recap

- Forwarded your message to other decision-makers

Score: 1–5
Indicates your story is sticky, shareable, and portable

How to Use This Scorecard

- Self-score after every demo

- Compare across multiple deals

- Identify weak spots (e.g., strong clarity, low emotional connection)

The goal isn't perfection—it's continuous refinement based on how the brain receives your message.

Section 5: Using Feedback to Improve Brain-Aligned Demos

You don't need more slides—you need better signals.

Most demo refinements focus on content: tweak the deck, shorten the flow, add a feature. But if your goal is to engage the brain, you need a deeper kind of feedback loop, one that looks at how buyers think, feel, and respond in real time.

This section shows how to use cognitive feedback or verbal cues, attention shifts, retention gaps, to build smarter, tighter, more memorable demos.

1. Debrief Every Demo with a Cognitive Lens

Ask:

- "Where did their energy spike or dip?"

- "What phrasing got a reaction?"

- "What did they repeat or write down?"

These micro-observations reveal what stuck, what skipped, and what needs reframing.

2. Test One Element at a Time

Run A/B variations:

- Change your opening metaphor

- Flip the demo sequence (value first vs. features first)

- Try a new objection-handling approach

Watch how each tweak changes engagement or recall. Log patterns.

3. Collect Qualitative Buyer Feedback

Don't just ask, "Did you like the demo?" Ask:

"What stood out to you most?"

"If you had to explain this to a colleague, what would you say?"

You're testing transfer, not satisfaction.

4. Build a Feedback Archive or Create a demo journal or shared team doc with:

- Quotes from buyers

- Common questions

- Successful pivots or stories

- Visuals that consistently resonate

Turns feedback into iterative intelligence, not just one-off notes.

The best demos aren't just delivered, they're designed, observed, and evolved based on how the human brain responds.

Appendix:

Appendix A: Building a Brain-Friendly Demo

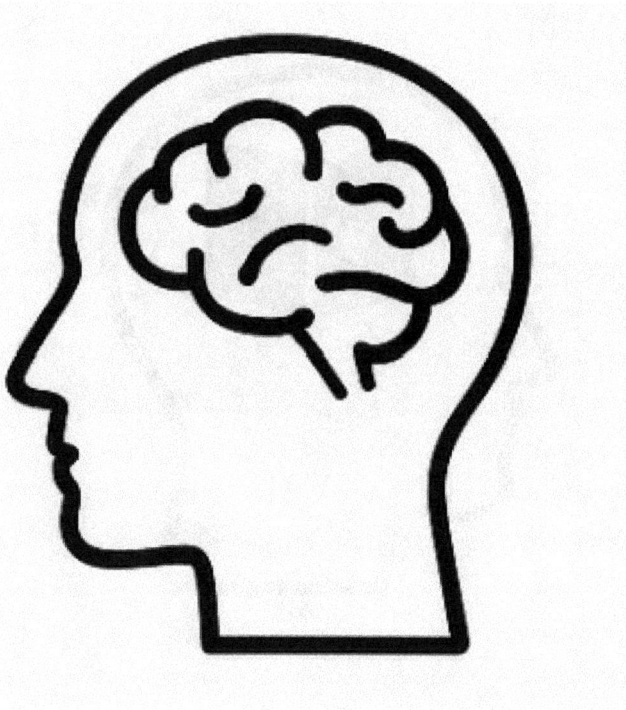

A step-by-step planning tool for preparing a high-impact, cognitively aligned software demo.

Demo Preparation Checklist

- Identify the audience's dominant pain point(s)
- Frame the opening story around a specific user or workflow
- Limit demo to 3 core ideas or outcomes
- Choose a metaphor or analogy for each complex concept
- Reduce on-screen clutter and emphasize contrast
- Plan "cognitive resets" every 5–7 minutes
- Prepare 1–2 visuals for each key idea
- Script your closing message and value recap
- Prepare your post-demo follow-up content in advance
- Rehearse with the feedback scorecard in mind

Appendix B: Framework Template

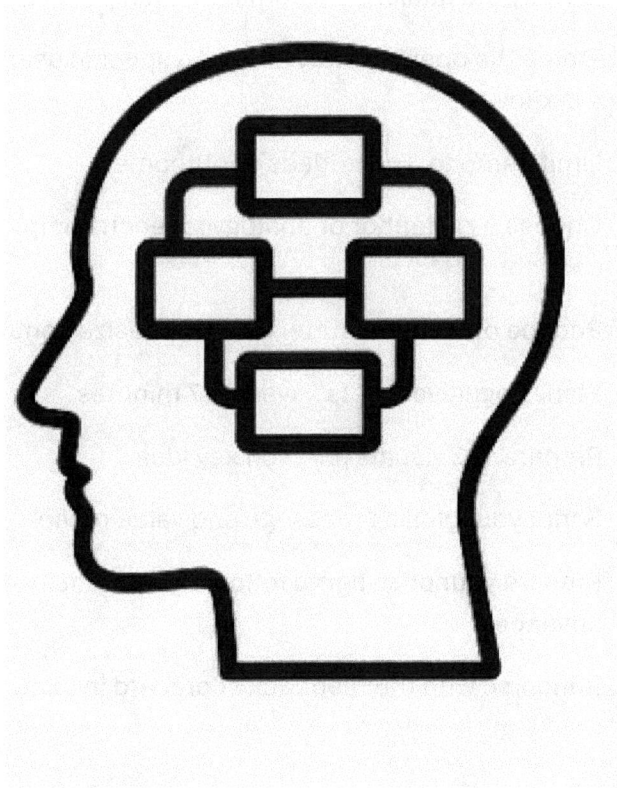

The 3-Step Cognitive Demo Structure

A repeatable structure to build every demo for memory, clarity, and motivation.

The 3-Step Framework

1. **Cognitive Opening**

   o   Hook attention

   o   Establish relevance

   o   Set expectations for transformation

2. **Memory-Optimized Middle**

   o   Organize in 3 main sections

   o   Reinforce key ideas with visuals and analogies

   o   Break pace every 5–7 minutes to reset attention

3. **Motivational Close**

   o   Tie back to opening pain

   o   Summarize emotional, operational, and strategic value

   o   End with a clear cognitive anchor and next steps

Worksheet: Plug-and-Play Planning Grid

Demo Section	Goal	Content	Visual Support	Emotion/ Metaphor
Opening				
Middle #1				
Middle #2				
Middle #3				
Close				

Appendix C: Sample Scripts & Slide Designs

Real examples for critical demo moments designed for memory and motivation.

Sample Openings

- "Let me tell you about a team that was drowning in duplicate claims…"

- "Imagine trying to fly a plane with three dashboards and no altitude gauge. That's how most teams manage intake."

Sample Closes

- "If you only remember one thing: this solution gives you control, visibility, and calm."

Slide Design Templates

- Side-by-side "before vs. after" visualization

- Visual metaphor slide (e.g., iceberg, bridge, map)

- 3-value recap slide: emotional | operational | strategic

- Next steps visual with simple branching paths

Appendix D: Recommended Tools

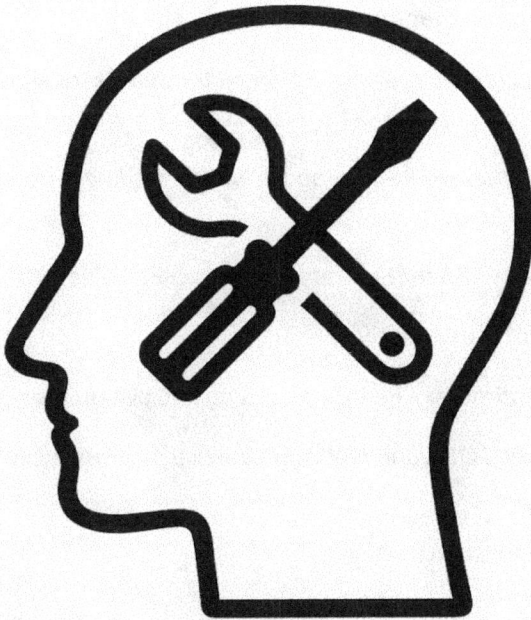

Tools to make your demo more brain-friendly, engaging, and memorable.

Annotation & Emphasis

- ZoomIt – On-screen magnifier and drawing tool (Windows)

- Presentify – Mac-based annotation overlay for live demos

Visual Design & Diagrams

- Canva – Drag-and-drop visual templates for slides and PDFs

- Miro / MURAL – Interactive whiteboarding for mapping workflows

- Loom – Record narrated visual walkthroughs for follow-up

Engagement & Interactivity

- Mentimeter – Real-time polling and live quizzes

- Slido – Q&A and polling inside live or virtual sessions

- Figma / InVision – Interactive prototypes for product exploration

Appendix E: The Cognitive Demo Quick-Reference Playbook

A field-ready cheat sheet for sales teams

This appendix gives readers a condensed "carry-with-you" reference summarizing the core science and tactics from the book.

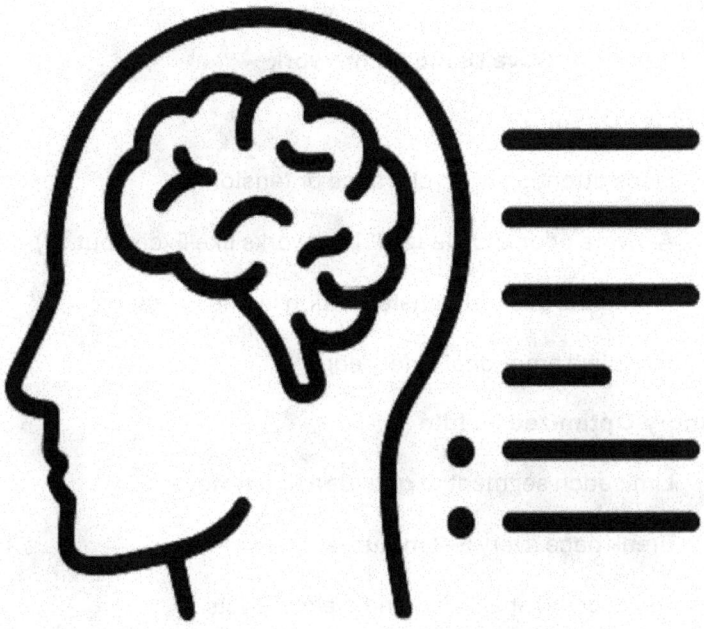

1. Cognitive Demo Principles at a Glance

The brain decides before logic does.
Buyers filter your demo through emotional signals, stress levels, attention limits, and familiarity. Build for neuroscience, not just narrative.

Perception beats reality.
If the demo *feels* simple, the product feels simple. If the demo feels overwhelming, the product feels overwhelming.

Memory is fragile and must be engineered.
Use anchors, repetition, cues, and emotional resonance to create retention.

---

2. The 3-Step Cognitive Demo Framework

1. Cognitive Opening

- Hook attention with relevance or tension

- Activate prior knowledge ("This works like Excel, but...")

- Frame the desired transformation in one sentence

- Establish emotional safety early

2. Memory-Optimized Middle

- Limit each segment to **one idea at a time**

- Break pace every **5–7 minutes**

- Use stories, analogies, and clean visuals

- Build mini-wins and emotional momentum

3. Motivational Close

- Tie back to the opening pain

- Recap: emotional → operational → strategic value

- Give one clear next step

- Implant a cognitive anchor or mental snapshot

---

3. Persona Load Map — How Each Role Thinks

Executives

- Wants: risk reduction, efficiency, time-to-value

- Avoid: technical detail, over-clicking

Power Users

- Wants: workflow clarity, familiarity, control

- Avoid: rushing, skipping day-to-day flows

IT / Admins

- Wants: integration, security, configuration

- Avoid: vagueness or hand-waving

Mixed Rooms

- Use persona signposting

- Segment into short cognitive blocks

---

4. The Cognitive Demo Checklist

- [ ] Did I simplify visual load?

- [ ] Did I speak to each persona's brain?

- [ ] Did I engineer memory moments?

- [ ] Did I build emotional resonance, not just logic?

- [ ] Did I use slowdown points strategically?

- [ ] Did I end with a clear cognitive anchor?

Appendix F: Memory Anchors & Story Prompts for Every Demo Segment

A toolkit of ready-to-use phrases, stories, and anchors

This appendix gives readers plug-and-play narrative tools that reinforce your frameworks.

1. "Open With Emotion" Story Prompts

- "Let me tell you about a team that was drowning in ____, until they changed one thing..."

- "Imagine logging in Monday morning and seeing ____. That moment is what transformed their whole workflow."

- "Here's a situation you'll probably recognize..."

---

2. Emotional Anchors

Use these at peak moments to prime retention.

Relief Anchor

"Most teams say this is the moment where the stress drops."

Confidence Anchor

"This is where clients tell us, 'I feel in control for the first time.'"

Identity Anchor

"This is what high-performing teams do differently."

Certainty Anchor

"If you only remember one thing, remember this..."

---

3. Visual / Analogy Prompts

- "Think of this like air-traffic control for your requests."

- "This is your before-and-after story in a single picture."

- "If your team used to drive with foggy headlights, this is high beams on."

---

4. Closing Story Prompts

- "Let me replay your transformation in 15 seconds…"

- "Here's the part your internal champion will retell for you…"

- "This is the slide your CFO will remember."

Appendix G: The Cognitive Demo Team Training Guide

A 30-day adoption program for sales teams

This appendix becomes an **internal enablement asset**, increasing the value of the book for orgs.

The 30-Day Cognitive Demo Training Plan

Week 1 — Foundations: Shifting to a Cognitive Mindset

Goal: Understand how the brain learns, remembers, and decides

- Watch/learn: Cognitive Load, Working Memory, Emotional Anchors

- Team exercise: Identify top 5 points in your current demo that overload the buyer

- Deliverable: "Cognitive Friction Report"

Week 2 — Rebuilding the Demo Structure

Goal: Reorganize demos using chunking and the 3-step framework

- Break your demo into 3–5 "chunks"

- Add persona signposting

- Record a dry run

- Deliverable: Updated demo outline + chunk map

Week 3 — Engineering Memory

Goal: Implement anchors and recap loops

- Insert 3 emotional anchors

- Add 1 analogical story per section

- Create a one-slide "Value Snapshot" for follow-up

- Deliverable: Cognitive Memory Layer added to demo

Week 4 — Decision Psychology & Conversion Moves

Goal: Turn your new demo into a decision catalyst

- Train on approach/avoidance cues
- Practice motivational closes
- Build a role-based recap email template
- Deliverable: Full cognitive demo + follow-up assets

Cognitive Demo Certification Exercise

To complete the program, team members must:

1. Deliver a 10-minute cognitive-opening sample
2. Deliver a 10-minute chunk from their real demo
3. Deliver a motivational close with anchors
4. Submit a written recap email

TOOLS INCLUDED

- Week-by-week checklists
- Recording review rubric
- Coaching prompts
- Team scoring grid

Appendix H: Tools

COACHING

CHECKLISTS

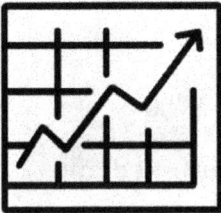

TEAM SCORING

RECORDING REVIEW

1. Week-by-Week Checklists

Implementation checklists for the 30-day cognitive demo program

---

WEEK 1 — Cognitive Foundations Checklist

Goal: Shift mindset from "product presenter" to "cognitive guide."

- [ ] **Understand the core neuroscience concepts**

  - [ ] Working memory limits

  - [ ] Mental models

  - [ ] Cognitive load types

  - [ ] Emotion-driven decision-making

- [ ] **Identify cognitive friction in the current demo**

  - [ ] Overly complex screens

  - [ ] Rapid context switching

  - [ ] Misaligned persona messaging

  - [ ] Feature dumping

- [ ] **Interview internal stakeholders (sales engineers, CS, IT)**

  - [ ] What customers misunderstand most

- [ ] Screens that create overwhelm
- [ ] Common objections tied to confusion

- [ ] **Create a "Cognitive Friction Report"**
  - [ ] Top 5 overload moments
  - [ ] Top 3 unclear transitions
  - [ ] Top 3 emotional resistance triggers

WEEK 2 — Structure & Sequencing Checklist

Goal: Restructure the demo with chunking and cognitive sequencing.

- [ ] **Break the demo into 3–5 chunks**
  - [ ] Each chunk = one problem + one workflow + one value
  - [ ] Each chunk names a takeaway

- [ ] **Add clear chunk transitions**
  - [ ] Reset attention every 5–7 minutes
  - [ ] Use verbal signposts ("Next, let's shift from intake to escalation...")

- [ ] **Create persona signposting lines**
  - [ ] Executive cue (strategic)

- ☐ User cue (workflow)

- ☐ IT cue (integration/security)

☐ **Draft an updated demo outline**

- ☐ Cognitive Opening

- ☐ Chunks 1–3

- ☐ Motivational Close

☐ **Record a dry run**

- ☐ Capture pacing

- ☐ Identify overload moments

- ☐ Note hesitation or confusion

WEEK 3 — Memory Engineering Checklist

Goal: Insert emotional anchors and long-term retention tools.

☐ **Add 3+ emotional anchors**

- ☐ Relief ("This is where teams feel the stress disappear...")

- ☐ Pride ("This puts your team in best-in-class territory...")

- [ ] Future-state ("Imagine Monday morning with zero escalations...")

- [ ] **Add at least 1 analogy per chunk**

  - [ ] Before/after

  - [ ] Story of a similar team

  - [ ] Metaphor ("This is your air-traffic control...")

- [ ] **Create a repeatable "Value Snapshot Slide"**

  - [ ] 3 bullet benefits: emotional, operational, strategic

  - [ ] One signature visual

- [ ] **Build a recap loop**

  - [ ] Verbal recap at the end

  - [ ] Role-based follow-up template

  - [ ] 1-page decision summary

  - [ ] Optional: micro-video follow-up

WEEK 4 — Decision Psychology & Conversion Checklist

Goal: Turn the demo into a decision catalyst.

- [ ] **Identify approach + avoidance signals**

- [ ] Approach: speed, control, clarity
- [ ] Avoidance: risk, complexity, unknowns

- [ ] **Rewrite close using neuroscience triggers**
  - [ ] Emotional confirmation ("This feels like the right path because...")
  - [ ] Identity alignment ("High-performing teams do this...")
  - [ ] One clear next step

- [ ] **Build the role-based recap email**
  - [ ] Finance summary
  - [ ] IT/integration summary
  - [ ] Ops or workflow summary

- [ ] **Final demo run-through with whole team**
  - [ ] Ensure pacing is cognitive-friendly
  - [ ] Confirm emotional anchors land
  - [ ] Validate the Value Snapshot
  - [ ] Get peer feedback using the scoring grid

2. Recording Review Rubric

A structured rubric for reviewing demo recordings with cognitive principles.

Use a 1–5 scale (1 = needs work, 5 = excellent)

CATEGORY	DESCRIPTION	SCORE
Cognitive Opening	Hooked attention, relevance established, emotional framing	/5
Clarity of Structure	Clear sequencing, chunking visible, smooth transitions	/5
Cognitive Load Management	No overload, pace appropriate, screens clean, minimal switching	/5
Persona Alignment	Messaging aligned to each role; strong signposting	/5
Emotional Anchors	Relief, future-state, pride, or identity cues present	/5
Stories & Analogies	Memorable stories integrated naturally	/5
Memory Anchoring	Repetition, takeaways, and verbal cues for retention	/5

CATEGORY	DESCRIPTION	SCORE
Visual Clarity	Screens understandable in 3 seconds; high contrast; simple layouts	/5
Engagement & Presence	Conversational, confident, checking for understanding	/5
Motivational Close	Clear value recap + actionable next step	/5

TOTAL SCORE (out of 50):

_____ / 50

3. Coaching Prompts

Use these prompts during 1:1 coaching or team training.

For Cognitive Openings

- "Where did the emotional hook appear? Can it be earlier?"

- "What pain did you surface? Did you make it feel urgent?"

- "Did you activate prior knowledge before showing something new?"

For Chunking & Structure

- "What's the one takeaway from this chunk?"

- "Is this a step or a chapter? How can you make it a chapter?"

- "Where can we add a pause or reset?"

For Cognitive Load Management

- "Which screen created the most cognitive strain?"

- "Where did context switching happen too quickly?"

- "What can we remove to make this screen digestible in 3 seconds?"

For Persona Alignment

- "Did each role get a moment of recognition?"

- "Which persona was underserved in this run?"

- "Were signposts clear and role-specific?"

For Emotional Anchoring

- "Where did the buyer *feel* something?"

- "Which emotion did your story trigger—relief, pride, clarity, curiosity?"

- "Can you name the emotional moment more clearly?"

For the Motivational Close

- "Was the next step framed as safe and easy?"

- "Does the close feel like confirmation rather than pressure?"

- "Is the value story easy for the buyer to retell internally?"

Bonus Coaching Prompt

"If they forgot everything but 1 sentence, what should that sentence be?"
(If the rep can't answer quickly, the demo isn't cognitively aligned yet.)

---

4. Team Scoring Grid

Use after mock demos, practice sessions, or real call reviews.

This grid provides an at-a-glance team performance view.

TEAM COGNITIVE DEMO SCORECARD

Scoring:

1 = Needs improvement

2 = Emerging

3 = Solid

4 = Strong

5 = Mastery

TEAM MEMBER	Opening	Load Control	Persona Alignment	Emotional Anchors	Memory Design	Close	TOTAL
Rep 1							
Rep 2							
Rep 3							
Rep 4							
Rep 5							

TEAM PERFORMANCE SUMMARY

- **Highest scoring pillar:** _____
- **Lowest scoring pillar:** _____
- **Pattern across team:** _____
- **Priority training area for next month:** _____

TEAM MOMENTUM QUESTIONS

- "Which chunk gets the strongest emotional reaction?"
- "Where do buyers consistently disengage?"
- "What single change would improve retention the most?"
- "Where can we implement additional memory anchors?"

Also by Jeff Mildon (MiltyMedia)

Nonfiction

Mildon, Jeff. *Infotainment: A Guide to Effective Sales Presentations*. CreateSpace Independent Publishing, 2013.

———. *Presentation Tactics: Objective 1 – Preparation*. MiltyMedia Press, 2024.

———. *Presentation Tactics: Objective 2 – The Mission*. MiltyMedia Press, 2024.

———. *Presentation Tactics: Objective 3 – After Action Review*. MiltyMedia Press, 2025.

———. *Virtual Sales Presentations: Navigating the Challenges of Remote Selling*. MiltyMedia Press, 2024. ISBN 979-8875717963.

Fiction

Mildon, Jeff. *Norse Star*. MiltyMedia, 2025.

———. *Spellbooks and Spaceships*. MiltyMedia Shorts, 2020.

Children's Books

Mildon, Jeff. *Artie's Color Quest*. MiltyMedia Kids, 2025.

———. *Cone of the Road* (forthcoming). MiltyMedia Kids, 2025.

In Development / Forthcoming

Mildon, Jeff. *Elysian* – A near-future interplanetary thriller.

———. *The Thwaites Protocol* – A scientific thriller set in Antarctica.
———. *Shadow Giant: Mission to Planet Nine* – A deep-space odyssey.

Discover more at MiltyMedia.com — explore fiction, nonfiction, and creative projects by

Jeff Mildon.

www.ingramcontent.com/pod-product-compliance
Lightning Source LLC
Chambersburg PA
CBHW030933220326
41521CB00040B/2290